Broken Homes, Borrowed Roads

This is a work of memoir. Some names and identifying details may have been changed to protect privacy.
Printed in the United States of America.

TABLE OF CONTENTS

THE BLUE HOUSE *5*

FIRST ARREST *9*

VENTING *14*

SECOND ARREST *22*

THE HOLDING CELL *27*

THE POD *32*

FIRST NIGHT *39*

SHIFT CHANGE *44*

BREAKFAST *50*

RECESS *54*

PUBLIC DEFFENDER *59*

COURT DATE *65*

LOST IN THE SYSTEM *77*

CASE WORKER *84*

VISIT FROM MY MOTHER *87*

SIX MONTHS INSIDE *96*

RELEASED *102*

THE PLACEMENT *105*

THE FOSTER HOME *109*

THE BLUE HOUSE WAS GONE *116*

SOUTHSIDE *128*

NO PLACE FOR ME *132*

DAVE *136*

THE QUIET YEAR *142*
THE UNEXPECTED BEGINNING *145*
THE TRUTH THAT BROKE THE QUITE *148*
TRANSITIONING *169*
UNEXPECTED HELP *182*
QUALITIES I NEEDED *191*
I STAND, I FALL *194*
A WOMAN WORTH *197*
CROSSING PATHS *200*

THE BLUE HOUSE

We used to live in this blue house deep in the neighborhood. It wasn't much to look at — paint chipped, porch leaning, windows breathing in more air than they kept out. The kind of house people drove past without stopping unless they lived close enough to know who stayed there.

But for us, it was everything and nothing at the same time.

It was one of the few places in my childhood where all of us were under the same roof. Where we weren't split up. Where I wasn't in some stranger's home, or some relative's living room, or lying on some extra mattress pushed against a wall. We didn't have much. We were poor. We struggled. But the blue house felt like a break in the storm.

It was big, too — two floors and a long fenced-in wooden backyard that looked bigger to us kids than it probably ever really was. In the summer, grass grew wild back there, tall enough to swallow legs as we ran through it. To adults, the house looked worn out. To us, it was space — room to breathe, room to play, room to be something close to free.

Inside, I had my own room.
Four walls.
A cracked window.
A thin carpet that didn't fight the cold.
But it was mine.

We didn't have AC, but I kept the window open every night, hoping the smallest breeze would find me. Sometimes I'd lie there and build different versions of myself in my mind — athlete, mentor, psychologist, somebody people looked up to. Somebody I wasn't yet but needed to become.

My mom was sick a lot back then. Not the kind of sick that ends after a few days, but the kind that pulls a person away from the world. She stayed in her room with the door closed, wrapped in sleep more than life. She drifted in and out, present but far. I didn't understand it then. I only knew she wasn't fully there.

Her husband — the father of my youngest siblings — was always on the streets with my uncles. He loved being outside more than being home. Walked around like the block belonged to him, even though the truth was the streets owned him more than anything else.

My siblings were young, trying to be kids in a house that didn't always feel stable. We ate what we could, when we could. Sometimes real meals. Sometimes whatever was left in the cabinets.

The neighborhood around the blue house stayed loud, messy, familiar. From that porch you absorbed everything — kids yelling, basketballs bouncing, old heads arguing over dominoes, cars drifting by slow like they already knew everybody's business. It wasn't just a place you lived in. It was something that soaked into you.

Summer days, the boys from the block and I walked to a big open field a few streets over. No coaches, no uniforms, no adults — just raw childhood energy with nowhere else to go.

Winter days were different. Cold enough to bite through your clothes. All of us squeezed into whichever house had a parent willing to let fifteen loud kids inside at once. Somebody's living room always turned into a whole youth center — laughing, wrestling, talking trash.

School stayed the only routine in my life that didn't change. Monday through Friday. Every afternoon when I got off the bus, my uncles and their boys were posted at the stop sign or leaning on our porch, laughing, hustling, smoking. Men who never clocked in but were always on the job.

School wasn't easy for me. My grades were rough, but I still showed up. Maybe showing up was the one piece of structure I could control.

ROTC became the one class I enjoyed. That's where I met Spinney. Light-skinned, skinny, always alert. Came from a rougher hood than mine. Somehow, we matched.

That's also where I met the girl I crushed on — the one who made the world feel lighter for a moment. One day in class, I asked her to the military dance. I wasn't expecting much, but she surprised me and said yes. We didn't have a car back then, so there was never any plan to pick her up. We just agreed to meet each other at the dance. I got a ride from family, kept my head down, and walked in like it was enough just to be there enough to be there with her that night was a great night but eventually that was my last night with her.

Nothing in the hood stays good for long.

Especially when you don't have a name just a kid with a dream to make it out one day.

She ended up pregnant by another guy from the block.
And Spinney… he didn't make it to that dance like we planned.
He was arrested a few weeks before — I didn't even know until I heard some of our classmates in ROTC talking about it.

The school talks, and a lot of us come from the same communities, the same neighborhoods — another kid with a record, trying to survive a world that failed him.
He went to jail.
Drug charges.

Gone.

And the blue house… even that didn't last.

I didn't see the cracks forming around me or inside the house. I didn't understand how fragile everything really was. Looking back now, the blue house was the last place I felt like a kid — before the morning the door got kicked in, and childhood ended the moment I opened my eyes.

FIRST ARREST

I woke up on a morning that feels so normal, I just didn't realize my whole life was about to change.

And it did within a matter of minutes.

I was lying in my bed in the back room next to the kitchen, radio playing low, window cracked because we didn't have AC.

Maybe you know that feeling—sleeping in a hot room and hoping a weak breeze finds you and gives you a little relief.

That was my morning.

Just quiet.

Just simple.

Just… normal.

My brand-new black Air Force Ones sat on the floor beside my bed.

We were poor getting something new I would just stare at it because it was rare.

My uncles had just bought them the week before for me from the booster who sold clothes and shoes out of his trunk.

Those shoes were clean.

Crisp.

Untouched.

I didn't know that would be the last moment they ever looked like that so soon.

Then—

BOOM. BOOM. BOOM.

The kind of pounding that shakes the whole house—shakes the air, shakes you.

My heart dropped.

My body moved before my mind did.

I jumped up barefoot, grabbed my shoes—didn't even tie them—just stepped into them, because every part of me screamed:

Move. Now.

My bedroom door was cracked open, and through that small opening, my whole world flipped.

One uncle sprinted down the hallway toward the kitchen. The hallway wasn't long, but fear stretched it out like it was never-ending.

And then the other uncle—

the one with the gun—

ran straight into my room.

His face didn't look brave.

Didn't look confident.

It was fear.

Real fear.

The kind that makes grown men act without thinking.

He shoved the black gun into my hands.

"Nephew… take this. Run."

He didn't check if I understood.

He didn't look back at me.

He just lifted my window and climbed out of it like the world was on fire.

My other uncle was already out the kitchen door by the time I reached it.

My shoes were loose, sliding, but I kept moving.

Fear didn't give me a choice.

When I stepped outside, both uncles were gone.

I didn't see my mother.

Didn't see my siblings.

Didn't see anything except panic and officers.

And here's the truth:

I wasn't running because I thought I could get away.

I wasn't running because I understood what was happening.

I ran because I was a kid

with a gun in his hand

and cops yelling in his yard.

I ran because I was afraid.

Maybe you've felt that kind of fear—the kind that takes over your body before you can think.

I ran up the yard, toward the front of the house, straight ahead.

My heart punching through my chest.
Shoes felt half on.
Barely breathing.
I didn't get far.
The officer tackled me so hard the world flipped upside down.
My hands hit concrete.
My knees scraped open.
My clean shoes scuffed instantly.
My white shirt got smeared in dirt.
The gun flew out of my hand.
Everything blurred.
My breath broke.
My mind froze.
The officer pressed all his weight on my back.
He was yelling, but I couldn't answer.
My throat felt locked.
I wasn't resisting—
I was in shock.
A kid in a moment too big for him.
And then—
I heard something that still haunts me:
My mother screaming.
A scream full of pain, fear, disbelief…
A scream I didn't know she had inside her.
A scream that tore through the whole block.
I still didn't see her.
All I could see were the officer's black boots inches from my face.
The entire neighborhood was outside watching.
Kids.
Neighbors.
People who knew my uncles.
People who knew my family.
People who saw me as just another kid sucked into something too big to escape.
Two officers lifted me up, stood me against the car, and patted me down.

They kept asking my name.
I couldn't speak.
Not because I wanted to be tough—
because I physically couldn't.
They put me in the back of the cop car.
And that's when I noticed my shoes again.
Those black Air Force Ones—the same ones that were spotless that morning—were dirty, bent, smeared with concrete dust.
I stared at them.
Not because I cared about the shoes,
but because staring at them was easier than facing the sound outside.
My mother's screams carried down the block.
Her voice cracked through everything.
Even inside the car, with the doors shut, I could still hear her.
I kept my head down, staring at my ruined shoes, hoping I could drown out the pain in her voice.
But I couldn't.
Her scream followed me all the way to the station.
At the station, they questioned me without my mom—something I didn't know was illegal back then.
They processed me like an adult.
Mugshot.
Fingerprints.
Paperwork.
Fear.
My first time inside a system built to swallow boys like me.
Hours later, they finally released me.
When I walked out, still shaking, the same uncle who handed me the gun was waiting.
He walked toward me with this look…
Like pride.
Like I had done something right.
"I bonded you out," he said.
Then he stared at me hard.
"You didn't say nothing… right?"

I shook my head.
"No."
And that was the moment everything changed.
His whole face softened.
He nodded like I had just passed some test I didn't even know I was taking.
When we got back to the hood, the neighborhood came out:
"What happened?"
"You held it down?"
"You didn't fold?"
Nobody asked if I was scared.
Nobody asked if I cried.
Nobody asked if I was okay.
They cared about one thing:
I didn't talk.
And for the first time in my life, people treated me different.
Not my mother.
Not my siblings.
Not the system.
The hood.
I felt noticed.
I felt respected.
I felt like I belonged.
But that was the dangerous part.
Because that day—
the day my uncles ran,
the day I got tackled,
the day my mother screamed—
that was the day the hood stamped me.
Not the police.
Not the court.
The hood.
And nothing in my life was ever the same after that.

VENTING

You ever go through something big and expect the world to stop with you… but it doesn't?

That's how life felt after my first arrest.

No pause.
No breath.
No moment to understand what had just happened.

In my neighborhood, moments that should break a person open barely made the block blink. People looked, whispered, then went right back to whatever they were doing — like trauma was just part of the background noise.

But something around me changed.

Not loud.
Not obvious.
Just heavier, like the air itself slowed down whenever I walked past.

Eyes followed me even when nobody said a word.

The police showed it first. They didn't ask questions anymore — they watched. Patrol cars slowed when I walked home. Windows rolled down just enough for eyes to lock on me. They stared too long, like they already saw me as the next case file, the next mugshot.

Even though my charge got dropped, it didn't matter to them. Paperwork said "dismissed," but their eyes said "criminal."

And the hood?

The hood reacted in its own language.

Boys my age nodded at me with that quiet, unspoken respect. Older dudes — the ones who used to look *through* me — now

looked at me.
My name had weight it never had before.

And my uncles?
They weren't proud of the situation, but they were proud I didn't fold.
Didn't talk.
Didn't break.

Where I'm from, silence is a résumé.
Silence is a reference.
Silence is a whole job qualification.

Before I knew anything about reputation, the hood gave me one.

I didn't want it.
I didn't ask for it.
But there it was — sitting on my shoulders like a jacket someone else put on me.

And the worst part?

It felt good.
Not good like joy — good like attention.
Good like finally being seen after years of being invisible.

Where I grew up, jail didn't make you a criminal.
It made you a story.

You become somebody worth hearing about.

And if you're a kid starving for belonging, the wrong kind of attention can trick you into calling itself love.

That's how the trap starts.

You don't know you want a reputation until the neighborhood gives you one.
You don't try to be "one of them" until people start treating you like you already are.

And here's the truth that nobody likes to admit:

The crime doesn't matter.
The code does.

The first question is never:

"What did he do?"

It's always:

"Did he snitch?"

If the answer is no, you're stamped solid.
Only then do the details matter.

That's why boys bragged about jail like it was some kind of trophy.

"Jail isn't nothing."
"I been down."
"I can do time."

They said it loud, like it made them bigger.

And the crazy part?

Jail didn't scare me.
Not back then.

Because when you grow up hearing about it every day, it becomes normal.
Expected.
Part of the story you think you're supposed to live.

The hood was the news.
You didn't need TV to know who got locked up, who came home, who folded, who held it down.

But all that talking comes with a danger nobody notices:

When you hear jail praised long enough…
when you see men go in and out like it's a bus stop…
when you joke about it with your friends…

Jail stops feeling like something to run from.

Until you're the one inside it.

Because that's when reality hits you with the parts nobody talks about —
the silence,
the loneliness,
the way time stretches,
the way your mind bends under pressure you never felt before.

Nobody tells the truth about that part.

And the beliefs that shaped me didn't come from one person.
They came from the whole environment:

Homes stretched thin.
Parents exhausted.
Kids raising themselves.
Girls carrying adult pain too early.
Boys mistaking survival for manhood.

When pain becomes normal, jail becomes normal.
When surviving replaces dreaming, the future gets small without you realizing.

And what happened with my uncle?
People think he handed me that gun to ruin me.
But it wasn't that simple.

He wasn't trying to destroy my life.
He was scared.
He didn't want to go back inside.
He didn't see another way out.

He looked at me — young, clean record, his nephew — and in his panic, I became the safest option.

He wasn't choosing to hurt me.
He was choosing himself.

And in the hood, that's normal too.

The youngest takes the fall.
The cleanest name carries the weight.
Kids become shields before they understand the war.

He thought I'd walk away untouched.

And on paper, I did.

But in every other way…
I didn't.

Because here's the part you need to understand before you judge that moment:

I wasn't thinking about the future.
I wasn't thinking about consequences.
I wasn't thinking about danger.
I was thinking about survival.

I was thinking about doing what my uncle — the only strong male figure I had — told me to do.

When your world is unstable, you follow the person who seems the strongest, even if they're leading you straight into something dangerous.

I was nervous.
Overwhelmed.
Fifteen.
Holding something I never should've been holding in the first place.

He told me to run.

And when you're that young, with cops outside the door, panic in your chest, and a gun in your hand…

You run.

People say, "I should've just put it down."
And I hear that.

But imagine the police rushing in and seeing a scared kid with a gun in his hand.

Do you honestly think they pause long enough to listen?
To hear a kid explain?
To ask questions?

Or does it turn into something worse — something that doesn't leave space for a book, or a future, or this moment right now?

That's the part nobody thinks about.
That's the part I lived.

And it's why everything that came next hit me the way it did.

Because even though I went home that day…

Everything inside me changed.

The system didn't forget me.
The police didn't forget me.
The hood didn't forget me.

Everyone looked at me like I'd been stamped:

"You belong to this now."

That's how a single moment becomes a direction you never meant to walk.

How a kid gets pulled into a cycle he didn't create.
How pain becomes normal, and normal becomes dangerous.

Meanwhile, home stayed the same — but same wasn't safe.

My mom, who begged the cops not to take me, shut down the minute I got home.
Didn't ask anything.
Didn't say anything.
Her sickness swallowed her whole.

Silence became her oxygen.
And I learned to breathe it too.

Her husband carried a darkness that filled every room.
He liked my uncles staying close.
He liked the chaos.
It made him feel bigger than he really was.

Inside that house?

Nobody talked about trauma.
Nobody asked how I felt.
Nobody even looked close enough to see what was changing inside me.

So I went back to school.
Back to the porch.
Back to the streets.
Back to pretending everything was fine.

Because where I come from, kids learn early:

If the adults don't talk about it, neither do you.

But life had already shifted under my feet.

The police watched me.
The neighborhood watched me.
My family looked right past me.

And somewhere in that mix — being watched, praised, ignored, and overlooked —
I started becoming someone I didn't recognize.

Someone shaped by pain, not intention.

And if you've ever paid attention to a storm forming,
you know the sky gets dark long before the rain ever hits.

That was me —
a storm building before anyone saw the clouds forming.

Where I grew up, the hood chooses you before you choose yourself.
And once it marks you, your steps start drifting toward a future you don't see coming.

I didn't know it yet…

But life wasn't done testing me.

And when the next test came,
everything would start all over again.

SECOND ARREST

It was a regular day — simple, quiet, harmless on the surface. The kind of day where you don't expect anything to go wrong. And maybe that's why it hit so hard… because it came out of nowhere.

I got off the school bus that afternoon — bookbag on my shoulder, sun still sitting strong in the sky, kids yelling across the block, life moving the way it always did. And like every day, I saw the guys on the corner by the stop sign.
My uncle's homeboys.
Older.
Known.
Respected.

Where I'm from, you don't walk past men like that without speaking. You can try… but silence becomes disrespect, and disrespect becomes drama.
So I walked over and dapped them up.
Respect.
Routine.
Just being part of the neighborhood I lived in.

But the second my hand touched theirs — police cars flew around the corner.

No sirens.
Lights flashing.
Cars moving fast — not cruising, not patrolling, but hunting.

It felt like they were already watching. Already waiting. Like the moment my palm met theirs, they wrote a whole story in their heads. To them, it probably looked like a drug deal. Maybe the older guys selling to me. Maybe me selling to them.

Didn't matter.
We didn't get a chance to explain anything.

They grabbed all four of us — three grown men and me.

I wasn't doing anything but coming home from school.
But that didn't matter.
Not in my skin.
Not on my block.
Not with cops who thought they already knew my whole story.

I wasn't being arrested for what they saw.
I was being arrested for what they assumed.
A kid shaped by the block.
A "product of the environment."
One more body the system already had space for.

They cuffed us tight — wrists yanked behind my back so hard it felt like metal cutting skin. They pushed us onto the curb, shoulder-to-shoulder, like we were all the same person.

The grown men started talking trash immediately — cussing the cops out, laughing, performing toughness like it was a talent show.

But let me tell you something only the inside of my chest knew:
I wasn't laughing.
I wasn't talking.
I was staring at the ground, trying to swallow my heartbeat.

But I couldn't show that.
Not in front of them.
Not if I wanted to keep even a little respect on the block.

The hood gives you a reputation you don't always want. But once you have it, you protect it like armor.

Inside, though?
I was scared.
Confused.
Sad in a way I couldn't admit to anyone.

And this wasn't supposed to happen again.
Not this soon.
Not like this.

The cops talked among themselves like they were building a story from pieces they didn't have. Then one walked up and asked my name. I gave it.
And my address.

And the moment he repeated it into his radio, everything shifted.
The walkie-talkie crackled.
He said my name again.
My address again.
Then paused — like something clicked.

His next words hit me hard:

"Oh… you one of them boys from the blue house?"

That was the moment I realized I wasn't being treated like a kid.
Not even a little.
I wasn't being treated like someone who made a mistake, or someone caught in the wrong place at the wrong time.

I was being treated like a file.
Like a stereotype.
Like a story they already knew how to read.

I belonged to the system now.
Not because of guilt.
Not because of evidence.
But because of association.

And that hurt deeper than any handcuffs.

I wanted to speak up.
Say, "I didn't do anything."
Ask for my mom.
Explain myself.

But hood pride — or hood fear — pressed my tongue down. And since I don't lie to you:
I was more afraid of looking weak than what the cops could do to me.

That's what growing up like this does.
It twists your priorities.
Makes survival about image instead of safety.

Eventually the officers came back.
No softness.
No curiosity.
Just routine.

They lifted each of us one by one and put us into separate police cars.

When my door slammed shut, it felt like someone closing a chapter for me — without asking if I was ready for the next one.

The ride took twenty minutes.
But inside my chest?
It felt like hours.

I sat in the backseat with my hands cuffed behind me, wrists burning, shoulders tight, mind unraveling. I leaned my head against the window and watched the world outside — kids on bikes, families grilling, people laughing, life moving forward like my life wasn't falling apart three feet away.

And then it happened.

A tear rolled down my cheek.

Yeah… the kid with the "reputation."
The kid who was supposed to be tough.
The kid who couldn't show weakness.

But alone in that police car?
I wasn't any of that.
I was just a kid.
A scared, tired, confused kid.

I turned my face so the officer wouldn't see.
Not that he was looking.

Another tear came.
Slow.
Quiet.
Heavy.

And staring out that window, one truth echoed in my head:
This wasn't supposed to be me.
Not again.
Not so soon.

The station came into view — brick walls, cold lights, a place built to take pieces of you. When the car stopped, the officer walked around like he was unloading cargo.

"Let's go," he said.
Flat.
Emotionless.
Routine.

I stepped out, wiped my face on my shoulder, and looked at the building in front of me. And deep in my chest, I felt the truth settle heavy:

I wasn't going home tonight.

Stay with me here… because everything after this only gets heavier.

THE HOLDING CELL

They didn't take me straight to the pod.
First stop was intake. A tall counter.
A computer.
A guard typing fast, cold, uninterested.

Stay close to this moment with me.
This is where a kid stops being a kid.
Right here.

He didn't look at me like a person.
Not a boy.
Not even a name.
Just another body in line.

"Name."
"Idress Johnson."
"Date of birth."
"01-12-1990."
"Address."
"1615 Savannah Dr."
"Parent or guardian."
"Jennifer Johnson."
"School."
"Northboro High."
"Medical issues?"
"No."
"Gang affiliation?"
"No."

And you can hear how flat that sounds.
How empty.
That's exactly how it felt leaving my mouth.
Thin.
Quiet.
Like the cold air swallowed my voice before it even reached him.

The place smelled like metal, old sweat, and fear trapped in concrete. I couldn't see what he typed — the screen faced him, not me. All I heard was the clicking of keys and my chest tightening with each one.

Let me be real with you:
He wasn't typing information.
He was typing my next hours.
My next days.
Maybe my next months.

Kids like me learn to hear destiny in keystrokes.

He finished without explaining a single thing.
Didn't look at me.
Didn't slow down.

Another guard appeared and motioned.

I followed him to the holding cell to wait for the magistrate.
The walk felt like moving underwater — slow, heavy, unreal.

They opened the door.

The room was freezing.
Four concrete walls.
A steel bench.
A toilet.
A vent blowing cold like it wanted to erase me.

And when the door slammed shut —
CLANK —
It didn't just close behind me.
It closed on me.
On whatever I thought I still was.

I sat on the bench, arms around my knees, trying to breathe normal.
Trying to stay whole.

Minutes stretched.
Time didn't move.
My thoughts circled the room like they were pacing too.

Through the vent, I heard the grown men they arrested with me — laughing, cussing, pretending none of it mattered.

They weren't brave.
They were practiced.
Good at hiding fear.

And the truth is…
I wished I had that skill.

Finally, the door buzzed open.

"Let's go."

They walked me into a tiny magistrate room tucked off the hallway — dim, tight, built for quick decisions, not justice.

Let me tell you something before we step inside:
This room decides kids' futures in minutes.
Sometimes seconds.
You don't get to explain yourself.
You barely get to breathe.

I stood at a podium.
A glass window separated me from the magistrate.

She looked worn down — not cruel, not angry, just tired from seeing too many boys like me.

She didn't look up.
She just read from a paper:

"You are charged with attempting to sell and deliver a counterfeit substance. Juvenile. No bond."

Those two words —
No bond —
hit harder than the cuffs. Harder than the ride. Harder than anything.

No chance.
No freedom.
No home.

She said it like she was reading a weather forecast.
A storm is coming.
Hope cancelled.

She slid a yellow sheet under the glass —
My name.
My charge.
My new reality.

"You'll be held."

That was it.
Cold.
Final.
Done.

She didn't even look at me.

The guard behind me said,
"Let's go."

No pause.
No moment.
No breath.

He walked me back to the holding cell.

I sat down again, holding that yellow sheet like it burned through my hand. My throat stung. My heartbeat dragged slow, heavy, stubborn.

I didn't cry —
not yet —
but the pressure was rising fast.

It felt like I was breaking.
Quietly.
Inside.
Trying to hold myself together while everything else fell apart.

And since I promised to tell the truth —
that was the moment I understood something:

The system didn't care who I was.
But I needed someone to.
Even if that someone is you.

Stay with me.
Don't look away.
Not here.
Not now.

THE POD

A little while later, the door buzzed open.
The officer stepped inside holding a brown paper bag.

"Lunch," he said, setting it next to me.

Before I tell you, what was in that bag, you need to understand something straight:
This is the kind of lunch they give you when they're no longer treating you like a kid. Or a person.

Inside was the same meal every kid in holding gets:
- A slice of bologna
- A slice of cheese
- Two pieces of bread
- An apple
- A small bag of chips
- A milk
- A water

It looked dry. Cheap. Tired.
Thrown together like it didn't matter who ate it.

But I still ate what I could.
I was hungry, and my stomach was tight from everything going on.

While I chewed, the officer asked me:

"You want to use the phone? Calls are free while you're processing."

I wanted to say yes.
I wanted to call my mom so bad.
I wanted to hear her voice and pretend for a second that everything was okay.

But I didn't know her number.
I didn't know anybody's number.

"I don't remember," I said quietly.

Let me explain that straight —
Kids like me say that a lot.
Not because we don't care, but because life gets chaotic, and chaos teaches you how to survive the moment… not memorize phone numbers.

He nodded like he'd heard that same answer a thousand times.

"Alright. If you think of someone, let me know."

Then he left, and the door closed with that heavy metal thud that made the room feel smaller every time it echoed.

I sat there staring at the apple in my hand, wondering if my mom even knew where I was — if she was worried, scared, calling my name, or lying awake hoping I'd walk through the door.

And I wondered something else too…
If the guys who were arrested with me would say anything to her —
or if my disappearance would just hang in the air alone.

Time passed.
Fifteen minutes… maybe more.

Then the door buzzed open again.

This time, he wasn't holding lunch.
He was holding chains.

Understand this clearly:
This was the moment where childhood fell off my shoulders.
Fast.

He didn't warn me.
He didn't explain.
He didn't raise his voice.

He just said:

"Stand up. We're moving you."

My stomach dropped.
I got up slow, trying to keep my hands from shaking.

"Face the wall."

I turned around.

He opened a drawer and pulled out:

- Wrist cuffs
- A waist chain
- Ankle shackles

Cold metal.
Heavy metal.
Meant for grown men — now being strapped onto a fifteen-year-old.

"Hands out."

I held my wrists forward.
He locked the cuffs tight and clipped them to the chain around my waist.
My hands hung low. Limited.

Then he pointed down.

"Ankles."

He locked those too.
A small chain between them forced my walk into a shuffle.

Then he slid a pair of detention slippers across the floor:

White tops.
Black soles.
Thin straps.

Cheap.
Flimsy.
Barely more than hospital shoes.

"Put those on."

I stepped into them.
Every step made a small, soft slap against the floor.

And that sound…
it felt like the system applauding itself.

When I was fully chained, he stepped behind me.

"Alright. Let's go."

Not beside me.
Behind me.
Close enough to catch me if I fell —
far enough to remind me I didn't control anything.

The walk from holding to the pod felt long.
Longer than it should've been.

Each step:
Chains rattling.
Slipper's slapping.
Echoes bouncing down the hallway like the sound belonged to somebody else's life.

Other kids watched through their tiny windows.
Some curious.
Some numb.
Some already used to the sight.

And here's something I never had the guts to admit back then:
My heart wasn't beating fast.
It was beating slow.
Heavy.

Like each beat was sinking deeper into something I couldn't escape.

Finally, we reached a big steel door.
He typed a code.

BEEP.
CLICK.

He looked at me once.

"This is your pod."

When the door slid open, it felt like stepping into a world that forgot what color was.

Grey walls.
Grey floors.
Grey everything.

Two levels of cells.
A dayroom in the middle.
Bolted-down tables.
Concrete benches.

Kids my age sitting around —
watching TV,
pacing,
or staring at nothing.

When I walked in, every head turned.
Quiet.
Studying me.

The officer led me down the lower tier, chains scraping the floor with each step.

He stopped at a cell halfway down.
Pressed a button.

buzz.
The door slid open.

"This you."

Inside:

A metal bed frame welded to the wall.
A thin green mattress.
A stiff white sheet.
A wool blanket that smelled older than I was.
A steel toilet-sink.
A tiny window too high to reach.

And on the walls, scratched in by other kids:

"Still here."
"6 more."
"Be strong."
"Why me?"
"Mom I'm sorry."

Those weren't decorations.
They were ghosts.
Ghosts of boys who felt everything I was feeling.

The officer stepped out.
The door shut.

CLANK.

That sound meant this was real.

I just stood there —
in the middle of the cell —
fifteen,
alone,
fresh out of chains,
trying to understand how my life had ended up inside a concrete box.

It didn't feel real.
It didn't feel possible.
It didn't feel like this was supposed to be me.

But the silence didn't care what I felt.
It told the truth:

You're not going home anytime soon.

And don't pull back from me now —
because what comes next only gets heavier.

FIRST NIGHT

The cell door had barely stopped shaking when the reality hit me:
I wasn't leaving.
Not tonight.
Not anytime soon.

No sitting.
No resting.
My body moved because my mind couldn't stay still.

It was cold — not the kind that sits on your skin, but the kind that crawls inside you and settles.
Even pacing couldn't fight it.

Thin white ankle socks turning brown at the bottom from the flip-flops.
Orange scrubs stiff, scratchy, useless against the air.

Breath thick.
Chest tight.
Tears running before I even realized tears were there.

And hear this clearly:
Crying doesn't make you weak.
In a place like this, crying means you're still human.

Time didn't exist.
No clock.
No rhythm.

Just pacing.
Just fear.

Then the thoughts came —
the dark ones.
The kind a fifteen-year-old shouldn't know.

Hurt yourself.
End this.
Nobody's coming anyway.

Words like "depression,"
"trauma,"
"anxiety,"
"suicidal ideation" —
none of those existed yet.
But the room taught all of them.

The light flickered every few minutes — buzzing, blinking, dying. Every flicker made the room feel alive in a sick way, like it was watching.

Let me pause the scene for one truth:
Jail doesn't just lock your body.
It locks your mind.

You think you're strong?
Think you've got heart?
Come stand alone in a freezing room at fifteen and watch your own thoughts turn into your enemy.

That's where strength gets tested.

The brown paper bag from earlier still sat on the bed.
Inside — a bottle of water.
Untouched.

Eventually, I sat down on the edge of the metal frame, picked up the bottle, took a swallow.

Leaned back to drink —
and the light flickered again.

Everything snapped clear:

This wasn't a warning.
This wasn't a mistake.

This wasn't a nightmare.
This was jail.

Something cracked inside.

I threw the bottle across the room, the bottle, slapping the wall, water streaking down like fresh tears.

Didn't care.
But cared.
Didn't know when water would come again.
Still didn't care in that moment.

Anger drowned everything.

Outside the window — black.
Night swallowing the world whole.

Pacing again.
Cold.
Angry.
Lost.
Lonely.

Every emotion hitting at once — shame, sadness, fear, anger, disappointment…

And behind them:
that whisper.

End this.
Nobody will know.

If you're young reading this, hear me:
One bad decision can open a door you can't close.
And once it shuts behind you, the darkness walks right in.

The wool blanket — rough, itchy, heavy — wrapped around my body.
Pacing until my legs weakened.

The mattress — thin, stiff, too small.
White sheet lifting at the edges like it didn't want to stay.
No pillow.

Finally, I lay down.
Not to sleep — just because there was nothing else left to do.

Eyes closed.
Opened again.
Every few minutes.

Each time hoping the room would disappear.
It didn't.

The cold remembered everything.
The silence remembered more.

Because this place wasn't built to hold boys.
It was built to break them.

And in that freezing pod, on that thin mattress, face wet from tears nobody talks about, a truth surfaced:

This room wasn't trying to punish me.
It was trying to erase me.

But exhaustion wins the battle that the mind can't.

My eyes grew heavy.
Breathing slowed.
Room fading.

Sleep came —
not gently,
not kindly —
but like collapse.

Not rest.
Not escape.

Just darkness.
Just nothingness for a few hours.

If you're still reading…
If any of this feels close to your life…
hear me loud:

Don't come here.
Don't even come close.

Choose differently now — before a night like this becomes your story too.

Because nights like this?
They don't leave you.

Ever.

And if you stay with this book…
you'll understand exactly why.

SHIFT CHANGE

The next time I woke up, it wasn't from rest.
It wasn't from sunlight.
It wasn't from anything peaceful.

It was violence that woke me.

BANG — BANG — BANG — BANG.

Keys slamming.
Fists pounding on metal.
Boots kicking doors.
Voices shaking the whole pod:

"SHIFT CHANGE!"

Before you think that's exaggeration, understand something clearly:
Fear wakes you up faster than any alarm clock ever will.

The whole row went off like an explosion.

My heart jumped into my throat.
I shot upright, blanket sliding off me, my body stiff from a night that barely counted as sleep.

Then another bang —
So hard the steel door rattled under my feet.

"JOHNSON!"

For a second, I froze.

Those seconds of not knowing what to do?
They age you and shrink you at the same time.

Was I supposed to answer?
Stay silent?

Move?
Not move?

In places like this, even breathing feels like a decision.

Then the order sliced through everything:

"ON YOUR FEET! OUT OF YOUR CELL!"

I grabbed my flip-flops, slipped them on, and the cold stabbed right through them like they weren't even shoes.

The door buzzed open.

I stepped into the pod — my first time seeing it in that grey, fluorescent "daylight."

Two guards stormed down the row.
One male.
One female.
Grey uniforms, black belts, heavy boots pounding like warnings you can't outrun.

"Stand at your door!"
"Back against the wall!"
"Feet together!"
"Eyes forward!"

Other boys were already lined up.
Different faces.
Different races.
Different mistakes.

But the same uniform.
The same fear.
The same silence.

And standing there, I realized something painful and honest:

We didn't look the same by face — we looked the same by fate.

Kids pretending to be men.
Kids wearing fear like part of the uniform.
Kids lined up like inventory.

The male guard read names off the clipboard.

"Johnson!"

My chest tightened.

"Idris," I said, the way we were trained.

He moved on instantly.

"Martinez!"
"Cooper!"
"Baker!"

Last names like commands.
First names like confessions.

No jokes.
No whispers.
Just boys trying to breathe quietly enough not to be noticed.

Then she came.

The female guard.
Slow steps.
Sharp eyes.
Scanning everything.

She didn't look at us —
she looked *through* us.
Through the fear.
Through the uniforms.
Through whatever dignity we had left.

She leaned inside every open cell door like she expected to find a whole crime scene inside a six-foot concrete box.

Understand this clearly:
She wasn't checking for danger.
She was checking for reasons to punish.

A blanket not folded right.
A cup out of place.
A piece of paper on the floor.

Anything she could turn into:

"No rec today."
"No phone calls."
"Lockdown."

Watching her hunt like that twisted something in my stomach.

That's when the truth hit me:
We weren't being checked on.
We were being checked off.

When she finished the front sweep, she walked behind the male guard, double-checking every door, every room, every boy.

Double-checking me.

And I won't lie —
I didn't feel human in that line.
I felt owned.

The male guard nodded once.

"BACK IN YOUR CELLS!"

No explanation.
No breath.
No mercy.
Just the command.

I stepped back into my cell.
The steel door slid shut, sealing me into silence again.

The chaos vanished instantly, like someone hit a switch and turned the world off.

I sat on the edge of the mattress, elbows on my knees, breathing slow, trying to calm the shaking in my chest.

Shift change.
My first one.

This is how mornings started here —
No sunrise.
No warmth.
No peace.

Just steel.
Cold.
Orders.
Noise.
Fear.

And after roll call?

Nothing.

No talking.
No movement.
Just waiting.

Waiting for breakfast.
Waiting for instructions.
Waiting for the next buzz.
Waiting for someone else's decision about your morning.

I leaned forward, stared at the floor, and listened to my heartbeat bouncing off the concrete.

And in that quiet, something rose inside me —
something sharp, something painful:

"This place isn't meant for any kid…
and it sure as hell isn't meant for you."

You don't know what it does to you to have your name yelled like it doesn't belong to you.
You don't know fear until someone inspects your life looking for anything to take away.
You don't know helplessness until your whole morning depends on what a guard sees in your room.

If you felt even one second of what I felt that morning…
you'd run from anything that leads you toward this place.

You'd drop the wrong friends.
You'd walk away from the wrong crowd.
You'd trust that voice inside telling you something isn't right.
You'd guard your freedom like it's the last good thing you have.

Because it is.

Sitting on that thin mattress, listening to my heartbeat echo like a warning, I understood something that changed me forever:

Nothing outside these walls is worth feeling this small.
Nothing.

And I pray you never learn it the way I did.

BREAKFAST

The next time the doors buzzed open, it wasn't a shift change.

It was breakfast.

Every steel door slid open at the same time, and the pod woke up like a machine switching on. Boys stepped out one by one — tired, quiet, rubbing sleep from their eyes — all wearing the same thing:

Orange shirt.

Orange pants.

White flip-flops with brown bottoms.

And that same cold air clinging to their skin.

No blankets.

No towels.

No personal items.

Nothing.

Just us.

And before we go any further —

Remember what I told you about places built to erase kids?

This morning is part of that.

The boys from the top tier shuffled down the stairs — some rushing, some dragging their feet — all of them moving like they'd lived this routine a hundred times.

I stepped out slower than everyone else.

My eyes scanned the pod, searching faces, studying expressions, hoping — even though I didn't want to admit it — that maybe I'd see someone from back home. Boys in my neighborhood bragged about jail like it was a badge of honor.

A small part of me expected familiar faces.

But I didn't recognize a single person.

Not one.

And if you've ever been in a room full of people and still felt alone, multiply that feeling by ten — that's where my stomach dropped.

We lined up as the food cart rolled through the door.

An older man pushed it — also dressed in orange — kitchen duty. His face looked worn out, like he'd been repeating this same morning for years.

A guard walked beside him, hand resting on his belt, eyes locked on us.
Trays came out one by one:
Cold grits.
A biscuit.
Something that might've been eggs.
A carton of milk.
Some boys sat down and ate immediately.
Some carried their food back into their cells.
Some started eating before they even found a seat.
Me?
I wasn't hungry.
Not even a little.
Shock sits heavy in your stomach.
It takes up the space where food is supposed to go.
The boy next to me — tall, scar over his eyebrow, eyes that had seen this place too many times — looked at my untouched tray.
"You want that, bro?"
I must've looked new.
Lost.
Shaken.
Still trying to understand what my life had become.
I handed him the tray without thinking.
Then I stepped back into my cell and closed the door.
I stood there with my forehead pressed lightly against the glass, watching everything.
Watching boys eat like this was normal.
Watching them joke.
Watching them argue about stuff that didn't matter.
Watching them shove each other, laugh too loud, pretend they weren't trapped behind steel.
Watching them live like this place was home.
Some shouted their sides of town.
Some cracked jokes like they were at school.
Some sat alone, faces blank.

Some looked angry — the kind of anger that builds inside you every day you're here.
But none of them looked scared.
Not the way I felt.
And since I promised myself, I'd be honest in this story, let me tell you something from that exact moment — with my forehead against that cold glass, watching life move on without me:
Fear feels different when you're trapped.
It spreads.
It settles.
It takes pieces of you that you didn't even know you could lose.
I stood there thinking:
Would my mom try to get me out?
Does she even know where I am?
Is anyone calling around for me?
Is this temporary?
Or is this really my life now?
That tiny bit of hope I had left —
Thin as a single thread —
Felt like it was slipping out of my hands.
When breakfast ended, boys drifted back into their cells.
Doors buzzed shut one after another.
The pod went quiet again.
Still.
Cold.
They weren't bothered by it.
They weren't panicking.
They adapted.
They accepted this.
They built routines.
They made this place normal.
And standing behind that narrow window, I understood something painful:
I wasn't like them.
Not yet.
Not even close.

This wasn't normal for me.
This wasn't home.
This wasn't familiar.
Not in any way.
But whether I accepted it or not, whether I was ready or not —
This was my reality now.
And I had no choice but to survive it.
And if you're hearing this — really hearing it — then take in this truth:
Nothing out there is worth waking up to a morning like this.
Not the money.
Not the image.
Not the "respect."
Not whatever you think you're proving.
You never want to watch life through glass.
You never want to see normal from the outside.
You never want to feel what I felt on this morning.
Once you do?
You'll never look at freedom the same again.

RECESS

A few hours passed in dead silence before the doors buzzed open again — that same loud, sharp, electric sound that cuts straight through your chest.

Before I could even lift my head, a deep voice thundered across the pod:

"RECESS! LET'S GO!"

The pod erupted instantly.

Boys rushed out of their cells like they'd been waiting all day.

Some wide awake.

Some half asleep.

Some already loud.

Some carrying yesterday's exhaustion in their shoulders.

Every boy stepped out wearing the same state-issued uniform they'd had on since breakfast — the same orange, the same cheap flip-flops, the same stripped-down version of themselves.

No individuality.

No personality.

Just inmates, not boys — exactly how the system wanted us to look.

And let me pause right here —

This is how the system breaks you first: by making everyone look the same.

I stepped out slower than everyone else.

Still overwhelmed.

Still confused.

Still clutching my paperwork tight — the sheet with my charge printed across the top:

Attempt to sell and deliver a counterfeit substance.

NO BOND.

Seeing it in my hand felt unreal.

Like it belonged to somebody who wasn't me.

The pod was already alive:

Board games slammed onto tables.

Checkers pieces tapping fast.

Football on the TV, boys yelling at every play.

Phones ringing.
Showers running.
Arguments popping off.
Laughter bouncing off the walls like it belonged there.
A whole world in motion.
And I was the only one stuck in slow motion.
I didn't want games.
Didn't care about TV.
Didn't want to pretend everything was normal.
I wanted answers.
So I walked up to the pod officers — two of them behind the desk, arms crossed, uniforms crisp, faces blank.
"Why don't I have a bond?" I asked.
The male officer barely looked up.
"You got to be patient. We don't know your case."
"What does that even mean?" I asked, tapping my paperwork.
"You'll find out in court," the female officer said, already turning away.
That was it.
No explanation.
No reassurance.
Just a brush-off.
And listen —
That right there is when it hits you:
Nobody here is going to help you understand your own life.
So I turned to the boys instead.
I scanned the pod until I found someone who didn't look angry or ready to fight — a kid leaning on a table, shuffling a deck of cards calmly.
"Hey… can I ask you something?" I asked.
He looked up.
"Yeah, what's up?"
His name was Monty, from the Northside.
Didn't know him, but something about him felt familiar — like he'd seen this place too many times already.
I handed him my paperwork.

He skimmed it fast.

"Oh yeah," he said. "You got to wait. Court date probably like two weeks out. Lawyer will come talk to you before that."

Two weeks.

Those two words hit harder than anything else that day.

Monty didn't stop talking, though.

He broke everything down like a teacher in a classroom I never wanted to be in:

"Roll call twice a day — every shift change.

Three meals — all garbage.

If you don't want your tray, give it to me.

Don't give it to the other dudes. I trade soups."

He explained commissary —

How family sends money.

How you order from a tiny booklet.

How soups become currency.

Bad deal — two trays for one soup — but I understood.

He kept going:

"One shower a day.

Phones cut off after ten minutes.

Calls expensive.

You need somebody out there who cares enough to put money on your books… because in a place like this, you find out fast who really loves you and who just said they did."

Then he asked:

"You got anybody sending you money?"

Like he believed I had a whole support team out there.

"…Yeah," I lied.

"Bet," he said. "Get behind me. I'll let you use the phone after my call."

But I didn't.

Because the phone area was chaos:

Boys pushing.

Boys yelling.

Boys cutting line.

Boys threatening each other.

Guards yelling back.
More shouting.
More chaos.
People fought over ten minutes like their whole life depended on it.
Monty stayed calm.
Played his cards.
Minded his business.
And eventually, he went home.
New boys came in.
Old boys left.
Faces changed every few days.
But me?
I stayed.
Waiting for court.
Waiting for answers.
Waiting for someone to tell me I wasn't forgotten.
Waiting for something that felt like hope.
Two weeks felt like forever.
But that was my reality —
Whether I understood it or not.
I was here.
And I wasn't going anywhere.
And before I close this chapter, I want to leave you with something I learned standing in that pod — holding paperwork I barely understood, watching boys laugh like this place was normal while I felt like I was losing pieces of myself:
This place doesn't just take your freedom.
It takes your sense of self —
Piece by piece, day by day —
Until you start forgetting who you were before the door closed.
So let me ask you something — honestly, quietly:
What are you risking your freedom for…
And is it worth feeling the way I feel right now?
Think about that.
Because I didn't.

And that's how I ended up here.

Not because I did something wrong that day getting off the bus. But because in this system, the saying is always the same:

"Once you come here once, you'll come here again."

And I guess the saying is true.

PUBLIC DEFFENDER

You think help comes loud.
You think when someone is assigned to save you, they show up like salvation.
They don't.
Sometimes help slides under a metal door like junk mail.
My lawyer didn't come during my first week.
The first time I "met" him wasn't even in person.
It started with a slip of paper.
A pod officer slid it under my door during lockdown and said:
"Johnson, call this number at noon It's your lawyer."
That was it.
No explanation.
No comfort.
Just a number and a time — like it was a dentist appointment.
But my heart jumped anyway.
For the first time since getting arrested, something inside me lifted.
Hope.
And I need you to understand this —
Hope hits different when you've been drowning.
It feels like a hand reaching down…
even if you can't see who it belongs to.
I held onto that thought like a life jacket.
Around noon, after lunch, they walked me to the phone.
My hands shook as I dialed.
One ring.
Two rings.
Then:
"Hello? This is your attorney."
My chest tightened.
My throat closed.
I gripped the receiver so hard my fingers hurt.
He didn't sound excited.
Didn't sound concerned.
Didn't sound like someone fighting for me.

He sounded busy.
Distracted.
Like a man checking items off a list he didn't want.
And then he said it —
the part he never explained at the time:
"I'm your public defender."
Back then, I had no idea what that meant.
So let me tell you what I learned.
And I want you to really hear this.
A public defender is a lawyer the state gives you when you can't afford one.
Sounds fair, right?
Except here's the truth nobody told me:
They don't work for you.
They work for the state.
The same system trying to convict you.
And in a place like that, you learn fast —
a free lawyer can cost you your future.
He didn't explain my charge.
Didn't explain what "attempt to sell and deliver a counterfeit substance" meant.
Didn't explain the consequences.
He just asked questions like he was reading from a script:
"What's your mother's name?"
"Your father?"
"Any priors?"
"Know their addresses?"
Half those questions cut deep.
I barely knew my father.
My mom was too sick to help.
I didn't even know what answers mattered.
The call lasted maybe five minutes.
Five minutes to understand my life.
Five minutes to shape my future.
Five minutes that changed nothing.
He ended with:

"I'll see you soon."
Then the line clicked dead.
Just silence.
And since I promised I'd be honest with you —
I felt like I had just spoken to a stranger holding the keys to my entire life.
Three days before court, the pod officers called:
"Johnson! You got a visit!"
My heart shot into my throat.
I thought it was my mom.
I thought she found me.
I thought she came to take me home.
You don't understand what that kind of hope does to a kid in jail.
Or maybe you do.
I needed her.
To explain things.
To ask questions for me.
To stand next to me so I wasn't alone.
Maybe my uncle would show up.
Anybody older.
Anybody who understood the system better than I did.
But when the door opened on the other side of the glass…
It wasn't my mother.
Wasn't family.
It was him.
My lawyer.
Tall white dude.
Long uncombed hair.
Black coat.
Eyes glazed.
Movements slow.
Honestly?
He looked like he needed help more than I did.
And let me tell you something real —
When you're a kid in jail, you'll take anyone who looks like they might save you,

even if they look like they need saving themselves.
He sat down.
Opened a folder.
Didn't smile.
Didn't ask how I was doing.
He leaned into the phone and said:
"Good news — I can get you out."
My whole body froze.
He kept talking before I could breathe.
"The prosecutor agreed to drop it down to a lesser charge."
I swallowed.
"A lesser charge?"
He nodded like it was nothing.
"Conspiracy."
I didn't know what that meant.
The word sounded bigger than me.
He didn't explain it.
Didn't break it down.
Didn't tell me what it would follow me with.
He just kept going:
"If you plead guilty to conspiracy, they'll release you."
Guilty.
For something I didn't do.
For something I didn't understand.
For a word I'd never heard.
My brain spun.
My chest tightened.
And he rushed me — voice flat, like he was late for lunch.
"It's the fastest way out. Just plead guilty."
And for the first time in my life,
I wished my mom was sitting next to me.
I wished she could hear what he was saying.
Ask questions.
Say no.
Say yes.
Say something.

But it was just me.
Just a scared kid.
Just a lawyer who didn't care.
Just a decision I didn't understand.
And all I could think was:
Home.
You'd be surprised how powerful that word becomes when you're locked inside a cage.
So I nodded.
"Okay… I'll do it."
Worst decision I ever made.
He closed the folder and stood up.
As he grabbed his things, desperate, I asked him:
"You're sure… right? I'm going home?"
He hesitated.
Just for a second.
Then he said:
"…We'll see."
And he walked away.
Didn't look back.
Didn't try to reassure me.
Didn't care about the fear he left sitting in my chest.
Back in the pod, I replayed it repeatedly.
He said I was going home.
He said it.
He said it.
I wanted to tell Monty.
But the next morning, after breakfast, they called his name:
"Monty! Pack it up!"
He froze.
Then broke into the biggest smile I'd ever seen.
"I'm out! I'm out, man!"
We all watched from our cell windows as he grabbed his stuff, shouting, laughing, bouncing on his heels.
I opened my mouth to tell him:
"I'm next."

But he was gone before I could speak.
And I was still there.
Still waiting.
Still believing a lie dressed as hope.
Still trusting someone who didn't deserve it.
Not knowing the truth yet.
Not knowing how far from "home" I really was.
Not knowing how deep the trap was set.
My lawyer didn't rescue me.
He handed me over.
And the worst part?
I agreed.
Because I had nobody to guide me.
And I need you to take this with you:
The system doesn't always take you by force.
Sometimes it convinces you to open the door yourself.

COURT DATE

Court was at 10 AM, but they woke me long before that.
The pod doors buzzed open so early the breakfast smell was still in the air.

An officer shouted:

"Johnson! Step out. Court day."

My heart slammed inside my chest.
Every step felt heavier than the last.

They lined me up along the wall right outside the pod.
I wasn't alone.

A row of boys — all in orange — stood shoulder to shoulder, quiet, nervous, staring straight ahead.

Then came the shackles.

Cold metal.
Heavy weight.

The officer tightened a chain around my ankles, then clipped a long metal chain to my wrists.
The chain from my wrists connected to the boy in front of me and the boy behind me.

We were locked together.
Like one long, slow-moving creature.

My ankles didn't just feel chained — they felt claimed.
Like the system had wrapped its hands around me and didn't plan on letting go.

Every step dragged a weight that wasn't only metal…
it was the feeling that I was walking toward something I couldn't stop.
A path already chosen before I even understood the rules.

And if you've never walked in shackles, let me tell you something
—
it's not just your body that feels restrained.
It's your future.

We walked in a straight line down a long hallway that felt like a tunnel.
Dim lights overhead.
The smell of bleach, metal, and old air.

Guards passing by.
Inmates pushing carts.
Some headed to kitchen duty.
Some being moved to medical.
Some already chained like us.

Nobody spoke.
Just footsteps dragging metal across concrete.

Eventually, they led us into a small holding cell —where they unchained us one by one
A cell that looked almost identical to the one from the night I was processed:

• white brick walls
• cold stone floor
• a metal bench
• one small window near the ceiling

Boys were already inside, waiting on their turn to face the judge.

The cold inside that room wasn't just temperature — it was a feeling.
The kind of cold that sinks past your skin and settles in your bones.

I kept rubbing my wrists where the cuffs had been, like maybe I could warm myself back into being human.

The floor was stone.
The bench was metal.
Every sound bounced around like it was trying to remind you:

You're not free.
Not even close.

We sat there listening for our names.

Time moved strange in that room.
Minutes felt like hours.
Hours felt like whole days.

My mind wouldn't sit still.
It kept bouncing between hope and fear like it couldn't decide which one was safer.

One minute I pictured myself walking out those doors, free.
The next minute a different voice whispered inside my head:

"What if you're not going home?"

I hated that voice.
But I couldn't shut it up.

It sat in my chest like a stone.

And if you've ever waited on a decision that wasn't in your hands, you know exactly what I'm talking about.

Finally, the door opened and officers came in with brown bags.
Lunch.

Inside the brown bag was the same processing food:

- boiled bologna
- two slices of hard bread
- a packet of mayo
- a bag of chips

• a piece of fruit
• and a water carton

This time, I had an orange and an extra packet of mayo.

The boys immediately started asking:

"You going to eat that?"
"You don't want that? Lemme get it."
"Are you done with that?"

One kid — older than me, quiet, calm — looked at me and said:

"You want that, bro?"

I shook my head and handed him the whole bag.

He said he wasn't going home today.
Not a chance.
He didn't even pretend.

There was something in his eyes — a kind of tired I recognized even though I didn't have the words for it yet.

It was the kind of tired that comes from life hitting you too many times, and you're just trying to breathe between the punches.

He looked at me like he didn't want to break my hope, even though he knew better than to trust this system.

I kept only the water.

While he ate, I told him everything:

• What the lawyer said
• How I was supposed to plead guilty
• How the lawyer said I'd be released
• How I was trying to believe it

He listened, chewing.

Finally, he said:

"You're going home, bro. If your lawyer said it, then that's what it is."

But something in his voice made me wonder
if he was trying to convince me
or himself.

I held onto my water,
held onto his words,
and waited for the door to open again.

Because when they opened that door next…
…it would be my turn possibly.

Name after name called.

And sometimes the longest walks of your life
are only a few steps.

The door opened again.

"Johnson."

My name.
My moment.

They cuffed my wrists — tight.
Locked my ankles — tighter.

And I kept thinking:

How dangerous can a kid be
for them to cage me like this?

On the walk to the courtroom,
my lawyer appeared suddenly.

Tall.
Long hair.
Black coat.
Eyes foggy like he hadn't slept.

My public defender.

People don't realize what that really means.

It means he works for the same system trying to convict me.
It means he gets paid the same whether I go home or drown in time.
It means he carries twenty cases in one hand
and my life in the other —
but he only has the energy to look at one.

He leaned in close and whispered:

"Remember what we talked about. We're on the same page, right?"

I nodded.

Not because I understood everything.
Not because I trusted him.

Because he told me the one thing
a scared kid cling to:

"If you plead guilty, you'll go home."

He opened the courtroom door,
and I followed him inside.

I looked for my mother.
For an uncle.
For anyone who loved me.

Every bench was empty.

My chest tightened so hard
I couldn't swallow.

The sheriff straightened up and called:

"Court in session. All rise."

Everyone stood —
me already standing,
hands chained,
ankles locked.

Then the judge entered.

A woman I had never seen a day in my life.
Black robe.
Calm, tired eyes.
Not unkind —
just burdened.

She didn't know me.
Didn't know my life.
Didn't know the mess I was standing in

Or how I got into this mess.

But in that moment…
she held everything.

She sat.
The courtroom sat.
My lawyer and I stayed standing.

She looked at me and said my full name,
soft but firm:

"Idris Johnson."

Then she read my charges:

"Attempt to sell and deliver a counterfeit substance."

A felony.

My throat closed.

She continued:

"You have been offered the opportunity to plead to a lesser charge —

Conspiracy.
Also a felony, though reduced in severity."

So you understand I was given a felony for a felony.

A lesser felony.
which was still considered a felony...

The judge asked:

"Mr. Johnson, do you agree to plead to the lesser charge of conspiracy?"

This was the moment
I needed a parent in the room —
a mother
who could look me in the eyes and say,
"No, baby, don't sign your life away."

An uncle
who could squeeze my shoulder and say,
"Think. Slow down. Don't take this."

But I had no one.
No voice.
No guidance.

Only a public defender
already closing his folder
like the hearing was over.

So I said the one word
that changed everything:

"Yes."

It all happened too fast.
Before I could even breathe,
before I could understand what I'd just agreed to,
the officers were guiding me out the courtroom door.

My lawyer leaned down and whispered:

"You're going home."

And for a moment —
God, for a moment —
everything felt light.

I thought about my mother.
My bed.
My neighborhood.
School.
My life.

Back in the holding cell,
I told every boy in there:

"I'm going home today."

They nodded.
Some congratulated me.
Some said I was lucky.

I believed them.
I believed him.

Eventually court was over for everyone "some went home. some didn't."

"They chained us back up."

They marched us back down the long hallway,
chains dragging,
lights dim,
the air stale.

But inside my mind,
one sentence played on repeat:

I'm going home.
I'm going home.
I'm going home.

Once we returned to the pod,
they uncuffed us.

The metal dropped from my wrists
and my ankles
"with a dull clink."

I didn't care.
I felt free already.

Before I reached my cell,
Glenn stopped me.

"Are you going home today, bro?"

"Yeah," I smiled.
"Lawyer said I'm out."

He asked for my tray.
I gave it to him.

Another boy asked.
I laughed and told him I already promised it.

I stepped into my cell,
and the officer slammed the door.

SLAM.

I lay on the mattress
and stared at the ceiling
waiting for the buzz
that would change everything.

Minutes passed.
Then hours.

Dinner came.
Dinner went.

Shift change rolled through.
The pod quieted.
Lights dimmed.

Still no buzz.
Still no officer.
Still no name called.

The day ended.
The pod went dark.

And the truth hit harder than any sentence:

I wasn't going home.
Not tonight.
Maybe not soon.
Maybe not at all.

The public defender's promise…
the boys cheering me on…
the hope I held all day…

All of it dead.

I rolled onto my side,
staring at the same wall
that had watched me fall apart since day one.

And the little hope I carried all day —
it sank inside me
like a stone.

LOST IN THE SYSTEM

The next morning, right after breakfast, the world felt different.
Not because anything in the pod had changed —
same noise,
same faces,
same cold,
same smells —
but because I had changed.
Because I believed I was leaving.
That belief was the only warm thing in that place.
I ate my tray — really ate it —
the cold eggs,
the biscuit,
the milk,
even the nasty fake sausage patty.
Because I told myself:
"You need strength, Idris.
You got to walk out of here today."
Every bite felt like preparation.
Every swallow felt like hope.
Repeatedly in my head I repeated:
Today is the day.
Today is the day.
Today is the day.
Hope has a heartbeat.
Mine was racing.
After breakfast, when things slowed down and the pod got quiet,
I walked toward the officer's stand.
My hands were shaking.
My throat felt tight.
But I tried to sound calm when I asked:
"Excuse me…
did anything come in about my release today?"
He didn't even look at me long.
Just scrolled a sheet with his finger and said:

"You're not on the release list today."
That sentence broke me.
Not cracked me —
broke me.
I nodded slowly and walked away.
My legs felt numb.
My chest felt heavy.
My eyes burned, but I refused to cry in front of those boys.
You can't show weakness in there.
Not if you want to stay safe.
But the second my cell door buzzed shut behind me…
I collapsed.
I slid down the wall until I hit the floor,
hands shaking,
breath shallow,
heart hurting in a way I didn't even know a heart could hurt.
That moment…
that feeling…
that crash from hope to nothing…
No kid,
NO kid,
should ever feel that alone inside a system built to punish before it ever understands.
My mind started spiraling.
I thought about the court date.
The judge calling my name like he was reading a file, not a person.
The public defender whispering lies into my ear.
The chains on my wrists and ankles.
The empty courtroom —
my mother nowhere in sight.
The judge reading my felony charges so fast I barely understood them.
Let me pause here and say something to every parent reading this:
When your child stands in front of a judge,
they are terrified.
They are confused.

They are overwhelmed.
They need you.
Because if you're not there?
A lawyer — a stranger —
will make decisions your child doesn't understand.
They will whisper things that sound safe
but are traps.
They will push pleas
because it's faster.
They will tell a kid
"Just say yes."
"Just plead guilty."
"You'll go home."
And your child
— scared, alone, desperate —
will believe it.
I believed it.
I was fifteen.
Facing two felonies I didn't understand.
Nobody in that courtroom protected me.
Nobody slowed down.
Nobody said, "Do you get what this means?"
So when my lawyer said:
"Plead guilty and you'll go home."
I did.
I didn't know conspiracy was a felony.
I didn't know it would follow me for years.
I didn't know it was giving the system more power over me.
I didn't know it would block jobs.
Block schools.
Block opportunities.
I didn't know it was
the beginning of a cage
the court built around my future.
I just wanted my mother.
I just wanted to go home.

And as I sat on the cold floor of my cell,
that truth
I didn't understand.
They didn't explain.
And nobody stood beside me.
To any parent hearing my voice through these pages:
Don't let your child walk into that courtroom alone.
Don't trust a public defender to protect them.
Don't assume the system cares.
Don't wait until it's too late.
Fight before they fall.
Guide before they slip.
Protect before they break.
Because I broke.
That morning, sitting on the floor,
I felt something inside me start to shut down.
I didn't want to talk.
I didn't want to move.
I didn't want to breathe.
I didn't want to live.
Not in that room.
Not with those charges.
Not with that lie.
I grabbed the Stephen King book the officer gave me —
the only thing I had —
and threw it across the cell.
It slammed into the wall
and fell open on the floor
like even it was tired of being in that room.
I paced back and forth,
trying to outrun my own thoughts.
I needed recess.
Recess meant phone calls.
Phone calls meant maybe reaching the lawyer.
Maybe hearing he fixed the mistake.
Maybe hearing the judge approved my release.

But before recess came,
I walked to the small window in my door…
…and what I saw
is something I will never forget
for as long as I live.
A new kid —
probably my age,
maybe younger —
stood on the second-tier walkway,
hands gripping the railing so tight it looked like his fingers might snap.
He was crying.
Not quite tears.
Not hidden tears.
He was sobbing —
loud, painful, broken sobs —
screaming that he didn't belong here,
that he wasn't guilty,
that he wanted to go home.
His voice cracked so hard
it cracked something inside me too.
I knew that pain.
I felt that pain.
And I knew exactly what he was about to do.
He turned toward the pod doors — his back facing me
his whole body shaking —
and then he leaned back…
and let go.
He fell.
Head-first.
His body hit the concrete so hard
the sound echoed through my bones.
For a moment,
every boy in every cell froze.
Silence swallowed the pod whole.
Then officers screamed:

"LOCKDOWN! LOCKDOWN! EVERYONE IN THEIR CELLS!"
Doors slammed shut all around me.
But I stayed standing at the window,
hands gripping the metal frame,
eyes stuck on the spot where he fell.
My stomach twisted.
My chest tightened.
My breath refused to come out.
hear this clearly:
That boy's fall wasn't just his pain.
It was OUR pain.
Every kid in that place.
Every kid the system swallowed.
Every voice ignored.
Every future damaged.
That fall was a mirror.
And in that mirror,
I saw myself.
I saw what I was becoming.
I saw what hopelessness does to a young mind.
I saw how fast the system breaks you
when nobody is looking out for you.
Lockdown meant:
No recess.
No phone.
No calling the lawyer.
No answers.
No hope.
Just silence.
Just me
and my thoughts
and the truth that hurt more than anything:
I wasn't going home.
Not that day.

Not soon.
Maybe not at all.
Days passed.
Then a week.
Then two.
Then almost a month.
Every day I tried to call the Public Defender.
Every day the call went unanswered.
Hope slipped out of me like air leaving a balloon.
Then one afternoon, the door buzzed
and a guard shouted:
"Johnson! You got a visit!"
My heart jumped.
Maybe it was the Public Defender
finally coming to explain everything.
Maybe it was someone from home.
Maybe…
Maybe it was my mom.
But when I sat in the cold visitation room
and the door on the other side opened…
it wasn't him.
It wasn't my Public Defender.
It wasn't my mother.
It wasn't family.
It was someone else entirely.
And whatever came next…
was about to change my life
all over again.

CASE WORKER

A woman walked in.
A case worker.
She didn't look dangerous.
She was calm.
Professional.
Soft-spoken.
Last name Gantt.
Too calm.
Something about her face reminded me of someone, though I couldn't place it.
She sat across from me, folded her hands, and said,
"I'm here to talk about your situation."
Like I was supposed to understand that.
And I didn't.
I didn't know what to ask.
I didn't know what to say.
My mind was spinning, and the only words that came out were the only ones that mattered:
"When am I going home?"
She blinked, paused, then answered gently:
"As soon as we find you a placement."
And that was the moment I knew—
I wasn't lost in the building.
I wasn't lost in the pod.
I was lost in the system.
And the system didn't care how long I'd been waiting.
"Placement?"
I stared at her.
"What you mean? What placement? And when will y'all find me one?"
My fists tightened.
My heartbeat picked up.
Pressure rose in my chest.
The worst part?

I wasn't angry at her.
I wasn't even angry at the system.
I was angry at the lie I'd been holding onto
the lie my lawyer fed me,
the lie I repeated to the boys,
the lie I believed because I needed something to believe in.
I tried to stay calm.
Tried not to use the word home.
Because deep inside, I knew:
If they thought I had a home to run back to,
they'd make it harder to leave.
She softened her voice.
"You will be released.
But not home.
You'll go to foster care.
Once we have a placement, you'll leave here."
Released.
But not free.
Not to my mother.
To strangers.
To a system that had already failed me twice.
She packed her folder and stood.
"Take care, Idris."
And just like the Public Defender.
Just like the judge.
Just like everyone else—
She walked away.
Leaving me alone with the weight of it.
When the guard opened the visitation door, tears were already falling.
"You, okay?" he asked.
I couldn't answer.
I walked back to the pod, head down, and went straight to my cell.
The door slammed shut.

This time, I didn't pace.
Didn't yell.
Didn't throw anything.
I just sat on the bed.
Empty.
Trying to accept a truth I didn't have the strength to accept:
I wasn't going home.
Not now.
Maybe not soon.
Maybe not at all.
Days blurred.
Pain became routine.
By my third month inside, everything felt like a cycle I couldn't escape.

VISIT FROM MY MOTHER

The letter came on a Tuesday.

Not a special Tuesday.
Not a birthday.
Not a holiday.
Just one of those long, dead, grey days in juvie where time didn't walk — it crawled. Where every sound echoed too loud because the silence underneath it was worse. Where the walls felt closer than they were and the air tasted like old metal and regret.

I wasn't thinking about anything that day.
I didn't have the energy to think.

I was sitting on the edge of my bed, hunched over, elbows on my knees, staring at the floor like the answers to life were hiding in the cracks.

Then the guard stopped at my door.

"Johnson. Mail."

Mail.

The word hit the room harder than the guard's voice.
I lifted my head like someone had called my name from a different world.

Mail meant someone out there remembered I was alive.

My chest tightened so fast it almost knocked the breath out of me.

He held the envelope out through the slot.

I recognized the handwriting before I even touched it.

Her handwriting.
My mother's handwriting.
Those shaky curves.

Those soft, tired strokes.
Those crooked lines from hands that didn't always listen to her body anymore.

I reached through the slot with both hands, slow, like the paper could break.
Like it could disappear.
Like maybe I was dreaming this whole thing and touching it too fast would wake me up.

I held it in my palms.

It felt warm.
Or maybe that was my hands shaking.
I pressed it to my chest without thinking — because before I even read it, I already felt what it meant.

It meant she was still fighting.
Still breathing.
Still here.

I opened it carefully, slow, like unfolding a piece of her soul.

Her handwriting spilled across the page like she was trying to stay alive through every stroke.

She wrote that she missed me.
That she loved me.
That she put money on my books so I could eat.
That she was coming to visit.
That she was trying to get better.

Her words were shaky, uneven, broken — but full.
Full of the kind of love that doesn't stop even when the world rips everything else out of you.

I read it once.
Then twice.
Then again.

Again.
Again.

Each time I read it, it hit a different part of my heart — the parts I thought had already died in this place.

That letter lived under my pillow for three weeks.

Every morning, I woke up, reached for it, unfolded it, reread it.
Not because the words changed.
Because I changed every time I read them.

At night, I slid it under my cheek like it could protect me from the walls closing in.

Three weeks.

Three weeks of hoping.
Three weeks of imagining her face.
Three weeks of praying she'd make it.
Three weeks of wondering if her sickness would win before she got the chance.

Then one afternoon, during rec time, the intercom buzzed.

"Johnson — visitation."

Everything inside me stopped.

My breath.
My thoughts.
My heartbeat.

Visitation.

Her.

I stood up too fast.
My knees wobbled.
My stomach dropped like I was falling.

I felt this wild mix of joy and panic — because when you've been disappointed enough times, hope feels dangerous.

The guard opened the door.

And suddenly I was walking.

Down the hallway.
Past peeling paint.
Past buzzing lights.
Past officers who didn't even glance at me.

Every step felt too loud.
Too slow.
Too heavy.
Too full of everything I'd been holding in for months.

Visitation is its own kind of fear.

You don't fear the guards.
Or the chains.
Or the glass.

You fear looking into the eyes of someone who loves you — and seeing pain you caused.

The guard opened the visitation room door.

I stepped inside.

The smell hit me first — bleach, cold air, old sadness that soaked into the walls and never left.

Rows of booths.
Thick glass divided each one.
Phones hanging from cords.
Fluorescent lights buzzing overhead like tired insects.
Faded posters telling you rules nobody reads.

And then I saw her.

My mother.

Sitting there.

Small.
Fragile.
Exhausted in a way that only sickness and heartbreak can carve into a person.

Her clothes hung loose on her body.
Her shoulders drooped like she'd been carrying too much for too long.
Her face looked dry.
Her eyes looked dim — not empty but worn from fighting battles nobody helped her fight.

But she was there.

She came.

She showed up for me in a place no mother should ever have to walk into.

I walked to the booth like my legs were made of glass.

I picked up the phone.

She picked up hers.

For a moment, neither of us could speak.

We just stared through the glass, two people trying to reach each other through something built to keep us apart.

Then the first thing we both said — at the exact same time:

"Are you okay?"

It broke us.
Just a little.
Just enough.

"I'm okay," I told her.

It wasn't true.
It wasn't even close.
But I needed her to hear it.

She didn't believe me.
A mother always knows.

Her eyes scanned my face like she was searching for the little boy she raised — and couldn't find him.

"You are eating?" she asked softly.

Not "Why are you here?"
Not "What happened?"
Not "What were you thinking?"

Just:

"Are you eating"

Because her heart couldn't handle the whole storm — so she held the smallest piece of it.

I nodded.

She still didn't believe me.

"How are you feeling?" I asked.

She looked down.
Her face tightened.
Her chest moved like breathing hurt.

She didn't answer right away.
When she finally did, it was barely a whisper:

"I'm managing."

She wasn't.
We both knew it.
She'd been sick long before I got locked up.

Her silence told the truth louder than any words she could've said.

We talked around things we were scared to touch.

I asked about the other kids.
Her face changed again — something between exhaustion and pain and guilt. She answered softly, carefully, like honesty might break both of us.

The whole visit felt like walking across thin ice — one wrong step and both of us would drown.

Fifteen minutes.

That's all they give you.

Sometimes I think the system likes it that way.
Fifteen minutes isn't enough to heal anything.
It's just enough to remind you of everything you lost.

When the guard called "Time," something in my mother broke.

She lifted her hand and pressed her palm to the glass.
Her hand shook as she held it there.

I pressed mine on top of hers.

Warmth through cold glass.
Love through separation.
Pain pressed into pain.

Her hand was so small.
Smaller than I remembered.
Weaker than I ever wanted to see it.

We held our hands there until the guard said, "Let's go."

She flinched like the words hurt her physically.

She stood slowly.
Her legs wobbled.
She steadied herself on the chair.

She forced a thin smile — the kind that tries to hide the fear behind it.

"I love you," she whispered.

"I love you too," I said.

She walked away — slow, fragile, tired in her bones.

Halfway to the exit, she turned back.

Her eyes filled.
Mine did too.

She lifted her hand in a shaky goodbye.

I lifted mine.

She held the doorframe for balance.
Took one last look at me.

Then she was gone.

The guard tapped my shoulder.

I didn't move.

My palm stayed pressed against the glass until the warmth disappeared.

Then I walked back down the hallway.
Slower.
Heavier.
Quieter.

Back in my cell, I lay down on my bed and stared at the ceiling.

Her face.
Her voice.
Her sickness.
Her strength.
Her love.
Her pain.
All of it stayed with me.

And the truth settled into my chest like a weight I couldn't lift:

I might've been locked up…

…but my mother was the one serving the real sentence.

She was breaking on the outside
while I was breaking on the inside.
And there was nothing either of us could do to save the other.

She loved me — deeply, painfully, fiercely —
but love couldn't fix this.
Not anymore.

Something inside me went quiet that night.
Not peaceful quiet.
The kind of quiet that comes from realizing the world is bigger than your pain — and sometimes that makes it hurt even more.

I wasn't going home today.
Not tomorrow.

Not until they found a placement.
And the system doesn't rush for boys like me.

So I lay there in the dark, wide awake, holding onto the only warmth I had left:

the memory of her hand against the glass
and the truth that she still loved me
even when life tried to take everything from her.

SIX MONTHS INSIDE

Time doesn't move in juvenile detention — it collects.
Days don't pass. They stack. They press. They crush.
And before I even noticed, six months had gathered around me like dust on an unused shelf.

Six months inside a place I never asked for, never wanted, never imagined… but still had to survive.

When I first got there, everything was loud inside me.
The doors slamming.
The guards shouting.
Shift change roaring like thunder down the hallway.
The cold that sat on your skin and sank toward your bones.
The boys fighting over phones.
The long silences at night where you could hear someone crying through the vents but didn't know who.

Then slowly… the fear shut off.
Not because I got brave.
Because my body figured out it couldn't stay scared forever.

Fear got tired.
Numbness took its seat.

The pod became predictable — a loop that never ended:

- doors slamming at dawn
- headcount

- breakfast tray you could taste the metal in
- locked in the cell
- recess
- lunch
- fights over the phones
- showers
- dinner
- lockdown
- silence
- sleep
- repeat

Every day the same.
Every feeling the same.
Every thought turning into a copy of the one before.

And reader… let me tell you the truth most people never hear:

This is how the system breaks a child — not with violence, but with routine.
Routine so heavy it crushes the parts of you that still believe in tomorrow.

After a while, the guards stopped saying "Johnson" like I was a threat.
It was just a roll-call sound — something to check off a clipboard.

The boys stopped sizing me up.
I wasn't new anymore.
I wasn't tough.
I wasn't interesting.
I wasn't anything.

I just existed.

And that's the real danger —
Not getting destroyed.
Blending in.

New kids came in every week.
Some crying so hard the officers had to hold them up.
Some acting hard but shaking under the act.
Some screaming for their mothers until their voices cracked.
Some already dead on the inside, just waiting for paperwork to catch up.
Some leaving worse than they came in.

You learn fast:
Hide what hurts.
Don't show fear.
Don't show softness.
Don't let anyone hear you break.

The yelling stopped bothering me.
The fights stopped shocking me.
The food stopped disgusting me.
The cold felt normal.
The silence felt familiar.

I used to count the days.
Then I stopped.
Why count something when nothing changes?

The hardest part wasn't the violence.
It was the waiting.

Waiting for the case worker.
Waiting for a judge.
Waiting for placement.
Waiting for someone to remember I existed.
Waiting for someone to say my name for something other than headcount.
Waiting for hope to mean something again.

Some nights I'd lie on my back and whisper into the ceiling:
"How much longer?"
"Why me?"
"Why can't I just go home?"

But I already knew the answer.
Home wasn't an option.
The system had a grip on me now — and when it grabs you, it doesn't let go easy.

So I stopped asking questions that hurt.
Stopped expecting miracles.
Stopped letting myself care about what tomorrow might look like.

My heart didn't heal.
It hardened.

And hear me clearly — kids don't grow up in there.
We shut down.
We fold in.
We disappear behind our own eyes.

The only thing that kept me from disappearing completely…
was my mother's letter.

Her shaky handwriting.
Her tired loops in the ink.
Her slow, careful words.
"I love you."
"I miss you."
"I'm coming to see you."

I read it until the paper felt thin enough to tear with a breath.
She was sick.
She was hurting.
She was barely holding herself together.
But she loved me in a way even concrete walls couldn't wash away.

And in a place built to erase you…
that was the one thing they couldn't touch.

Six months.
Six months of surviving boys who broke in silence.
Six months of becoming quieter, harder, colder.
Six months of waking up to a world that didn't care if I came out better or worse.

Six months waiting for a placement that would never feel like home.
Six months learning the truth about systems made for kids like me:

They don't fix you.
They don't heal you.
They don't teach you anything except how to stop feeling things that should hurt.

Six months inside…
and I wasn't the same boy anymore.

And before we step into the next chapter, I need to say this to you — not from a cell, not from fear, but from memory:

You have no idea how fast life can swallow a kid who wasn't prepared.
How quickly innocence can be replaced by survival.
How easily a moment can become a direction.
How routine can become a cage.
How a cage can become normal.
And how normal can make you forget you were ever meant for something else.

My younger self sits in that memory — knees pulled in, back against cold brick, breathing like air costs money.

I look back and remember those times and says one thing:
"Six months felt like six years."

I look back now — older, clearer, stronger — the voice I didn't know I would grow into.

And I tell you what I wish someone had told me:

Sometimes strength isn't loud.
Sometimes strength is just staying alive long enough to reach the door that finally opens.

You might never sit in a cell like that.
And I pray you never will.

But if life ever cages you —
in fear,
in pressure,
in pain,
in confusion —
remember this chapter.

Remember the boy I was.
Remember what silence did to me.
Remember what survival felt like.
Remember the cost of one decision made too fast.

Hold that wisdom like a key.

And in the next chapter…

…I finally walk out.

RELEASED

They called my name in the cell, sharp enough to break through the silence I had been living in.
For a second, I didn't move.

You learn in places like that not to react too fast — names can mean bad news, more waiting, or another round of questions. But the officer repeated it, louder this time:

"Get your things. You're being released."

My heart jumped, but my mind froze.

Released?
Was my mother outside?
Was I finally going home?

I stood up slowly, following the officer down the hallway toward processing, where freedom had to wait behind paperwork and cold benches.

They sat me on a hard seat under buzzing lights.
The air felt stale.
My thoughts were running too fast to grab.

Then they brought out my property bag — the clear sack holding everything I came in with. It looked small in the officer's hands, like my whole life barely took up any space.

"Sign here," he said.

My hand trembled slightly as I signed. Not from fear — from the unknown waiting behind those doors.

They walked me down the final hallway.
Doors buzzed.
Doors slammed.
Each one sounded like a chapter closing behind me.

When I stepped into the lobby, sunlight hit my eyes, and I saw her:

The case worker.

This wasn't the first time I'd seen her — it was the second.
Enough to remember her voice.
Enough to remember she wasn't the smiling type.

Calm.
Straightforward.
Unreadable.

"Come on," she said.

But she didn't walk straight to her car. She stopped, looked at me for a moment, and asked:

"You hungry?"

I nodded.

My stomach was empty, but the confusion in my chest was louder.
Why was she here instead of my mother?
Where was I going?
What was happening now?

She led me across the street to a small restaurant the kind of place people stop at before work. The smell of food hit me hard — reminding me how long it had been since I had a warm meal.

We sat in a booth by the window.
She ordered for both of us.
I didn't say much.
Barely looked around.

When the food came, I ate slowly, still trying to understand what my life had just turned into.

As I ate, she talked in that calm, controlled tone:

"You won't be going home today."
"You'll be going into a foster placement."
"It's temporary. Until things get sorted."

Sorted.
Placement.
Temporary.

Words that mean you don't get a choice.

She watched me finish eating, then asked the restaurant worker:

"Can we get some of that to go?"

She handed me the small bag of extra food — not from warmth, not from care, but because she knew I had nothing waiting for me wherever she was taking me.

We walked to the car.
I held the bag tight.
She didn't ask how I felt.
Didn't ask if I wanted to see my mother.
Didn't ask anything personal.

She just drove.

And as the building disappeared behind us, something settled deep inside me:

This wasn't the beginning of foster care.
This was foster care **again**.

Another house.
Another placement.
Another set of rules.
Another round of survival.

And the road we were on — silent, long, and heavy — was carrying me straight into the next chapter of my life, whether I was ready or not.

THE PLACEMENT

We drove to the Child Protective Services building; the place kids go when the state is about to redraw their whole world.
No cuffs.
No charges.
Just that cold kind of paperwork that decides where you sleep next.

Inside, she led me past the quiet lobby and into hallways I had never seen before — polished floors, bright lights, motivational posters that didn't motivate anyone.

She opened a door to the back office.

That's when I saw it:

A giant room of cubicles — rows and rows of small boxes where adults-built futures for kids like me on computer screens.

Walking through that room felt like walking through a factory where destinies were assembled in pieces.

Her cubicle was too neat for someone who handled chaos daily:

Papers stacked tight.
A bright green plant.
A mug with her name on it.
Pictures covering the wall — vacations, birthdays, graduations, dogs in sweaters, family smiles.

A wall full of everything I never had.

"Have a seat," she said.

I sat slow, unsure — my Black Air Forces sinking into carpet too clean for shoes like mine.

She logged into her computer and started typing.
Every keystroke felt like a countdown.

Then the questions came:

"Where were you staying after your first arrest?"
"Who bonded you out?"
"How long were you gone before the second arrest?"
"Did anyone know where you were living?"

I lied.
Calm.
Straight-faced.

Not to deceive — but to protect the people who tried to keep me afloat, even imperfectly.

She typed, giving the same script I'd heard before:

"…additional violations…"
"…failed placements…"
"…supervision increases…"
"…the impact of running…"

Her voice faded in and out, like she had said this a thousand times.

My eyes drifted toward her pictures again.

And then something hit me so hard I forgot how to breathe.

Because mixed in with all those smiling faces…
was a picture of me.

Me in ninth-grade ROTC military uniform.
Me standing next to a girl in a shimmering dress.
Me before life swallowed me whole.

I stared until I finally said:

"Um… that's me."

She turned, blinked, leaned closer, and laughed — soft, surprised.

"Oh! You're right. That is, you."

She tucked a strand of hair behind her ear.

"That's my sister. You two went to the dance together?"

I nodded.

But inside me, something else moved — something I hadn't felt in a long time:

Hope.
Or the memory of it.

For a moment, I thought:

Maybe this means something.
Maybe she sees me.
Maybe I'm not just a file.
Maybe…

But she turned back to her keyboard and kept typing like nothing happened.

No curiosity.
No warmth.
No pause.

And something settled inside me:

Connections don't matter in the system.
People don't follow you from room to room.
Care doesn't travel.

After a few minutes she stood.

"Alright, Idris. They're ready for you."

Just like that.

We walked out of the cubicle maze — her heels tapping steady, me behind her in shoes that had walked through too many temporary lives already.

Outside, sunlight hit me like it didn't recognize me anymore.

She opened the driver's door.
I got into the passenger seat.

Whatever that picture stirred inside me — she left it behind instantly.

And I know she would disappear from my life the way every adult in the system disappeared after she dropped me off:

Not slowly.
Not dramatically.
Just completely.

Without leaving a single piece of herself behind.

And as the car pulled off toward the foster home — a place that wouldn't feel like home — something tightened in my chest:

Whatever waited behind those doors…
whatever rules, silence, routines, or strangers…
I'd be facing it alone again.

But this time, I understood the truth:

Walking into a foster home blind is one thing.
Walking in knowing exactly what the system turns you into…
is heavier.

THE FOSTER HOME

The foster home was on the total opposite side of town —
far enough that it didn't even feel like my city anymore.
This wasn't the blue house.
This wasn't my neighborhood.
This wasn't anything familiar.
It felt like being relocated to a version of life where nobody knew my name —
and nobody cared to learn it.

When the case worker pulled up, she didn't say much.
She unbuckled her seatbelt.
Stepped out.
Motioned for me to follow.

The woman who answered the door looked older than the walls behind her —
grey hair pulled tight like she didn't trust it to fall,
glasses halfway down her nose,
skin worn thin from years that didn't soften her — they sharpened her.

There was a smell in the house.
Not dirty.
Not rotten.
Just… old.
Like the house had collected time and never bothered to release it.

She greets me.
Didn't ask how I was.
Didn't ask where I came from.

"Your rooms down the hall," she said.
"You're sharing."

That was it.
That was my welcome.

The living room was crowded with old furniture and stacks of magazines that looked like they hadn't been touched in years. Heavy curtains blocked sunlight like the house didn't want witnesses.

The case worker walked me down the hallway, pointing at things like she was reading instructions off a form.

Bathroom.
Kitchen.
Bedroom.

Her voice was stiff. Controlled. Distant.
Not like the car ride.
And I knew why.

After the picture in her cubicle.
After she realized I had once taken her sister to the military dance.
After she connected who I used to be…
to who I was now.

I wasn't the boy in the photo anymore.
I was a file.
A case.
A ward of the state.
Someone she didn't want to touch her real world.

"I'll check on you soon," she said.

But I already knew she wouldn't.
And she didn't.

That was the last time I saw her.

The boy in the room was already sitting on his bed when I walked in.
Tall. Light-skinned. Quiet — but not weak quiet. Controlled quiet.
He looked at me like he had already measured the situation.

"John," he said.
No smile. No judgment.

Straight face
with introduction.

"You'll get used to this place," he added.
"It's better than most."

Better than most.
That sentence told me everything I needed to know about how low the standard was.
Some kids had it worse.
Some kids were in houses where "better than most" meant something different.

The room had two small beds. Thin blankets. Springs that complained when you moved. A window that barely opened.

It wasn't a bedroom.
It was a holding cell without bars.

The foster lady didn't care what we did.
She didn't:

- ask where we went
- check homework
- ask about school
- make sure we had clothes
- cook unless required
- check if we were safe

If nothing got broken
and the money kept coming,
she was satisfied.

John understood that long before I arrived.

"Don't expect anything," he told me one night while staring at the ceiling.
"Then you won't be disappointed."

He didn't say it angry.
He said it practiced.

After a few days, I was transferred to a small school down the street.
No ROTC.
No familiar faces.
No connection.

I stayed quiet.
Did my work.
Watched the clock.
Counted the days.
Counted how far it would be to walk back to the blue house.

Every day felt temporary.

John noticed.

One day he asked me.

"You still thinking about going back?"

"Yea, I said.

"You think it's waiting?"

That question stuck deeper than he meant for it to.

John was to his self quite focus not a talker but an inviter at least with me he was that way.

He use to invite me to the skating ring telling me it felt like freedom moving around that circle wooden floor on them skates as fast as you could go to him that was freedom.

John skated a lot and that's the only place John looked different was outside that house.
At the skating rink, he moved like gravity worked for him.
Smooth. Confident. Like the system didn't own him.

He took me with him sometimes.
At first, I watched.
Then I tried.
I fell.
Got back up.
Fell again.

But for the first time in months, I felt something that didn't feel like survival.

At the rink:

- nobody knew I came from detention
- nobody knew I was in foster care
- nobody saw me as broken

I was just another kid trying not to fall.

But the moment we walked back into that old house, the feeling left.
The weight returned.

Months passed.
The case worker never came back.
Not once.

And I believed — and still believe — she avoided my case because of her sister.
Because she saw me in that picture.
Because she didn't want her real life touching her job life.

She didn't know my story.
She didn't know what led me there.
She didn't know I wasn't a monster.
But she pulled away anyway.

And when you're a kid, silence feels personal.

I lasted a few months in that house.
A few months of skating.
A few months of sneaking out at night.
A few months of visiting my thoughts of my plan to go home.

Every time I came back to the foster home, it felt heavier.
Like I was shrinking inside it.

I knew the foster lady didn't care.
I knew the system had no plan for me.
I knew the case worker wasn't coming back.

John knew something too.

"You're not staying," he said one night.

"No."

"You sure it's still there?"

I didn't answer.
Because I didn't know.

The house was quiet.
Too quiet.
That kind of quiet where the walls feel like they're listening.

I sat on the edge of the bed, tying my shoes.
John sat up slowly.

"You're going," he said — not a question.

"Yea."

He looked toward the hallway.
"You sure this isn't you just running?"

I swallowed.
"I have to know."

He rubbed his face.

"I would go" but "I can't go."
No bitterness.
No jealousy.

"This place isn't good," he said, glancing around the dim room, "but it's the only roof I got."

He meant it.
That was his reality.
A bad roof was still a roof.

Then he looked at me one more time.

"If she hears you, it's done."

That was all he could offer.

I moved down the hallway slowly.
No speeches.
No goodbye hug.
Just a boy trying not to let the floor creak.

The door clicked shut behind me.
John stayed in that room.

And for the first time, leaving didn't feel powerful.
It felt like losing the only steady thing that house gave me.

THE BLUE HOUSE WAS GONE

After I walked away from the foster house that night, there was no going back.
Not to that room.
Not to John.
Not to the old lady's hallway.

Once I stepped off that porch and into the street, I wasn't a placement anymore.
I was just out there.

My mind was already set — I was going back to the blue house.

I walked the long route back, expecting to see the same chipped blue paint, the same porch with its uneven steps, the same familiar noise drifting from inside.
In my head, it was still alive.
Still mine.

I walk down the sidewalk toward the blue house —
The closer I get, the tighter my chest feels.

I knock.
Once.
Twice.
Three times.

Nothing.

I knock again — softer this time.
Like maybe the house is sleeping and I don't want to wake it too hard.

Still nothing.

I try the handle.
Locked.

I look through the window.

Empty.

No couch.
No table.
No curtains.

They moved.
And nobody told me.

So I just stood there, staring at the door as if it would open — as if someone might suddenly appear and tell me it was all a mistake.

Cars pass.
People laugh down the street.
Life doesn't pause for lost kids.

I sit on the porch facing the street.
Not the house.
The street.

I stare at my black Air Forces — scraped from the night the cops tackled me.

"My whole life…" I say slowly,
"I've just been trying to get back home."

Not to be hard.
Not to survive.
Not to become this.

"I just wanted my mom. My brothers and sisters. My old room."

Everything was gone.

"You ever chase something because you think it's still waiting?"

I shake my head.

"And when you get there…"
I swallow.
"It's gone."

John's voice echoes in my head:
"You are leaving for something… or just from something?"

Sitting on that porch, I finally understand.
I wasn't running toward home.
I was running from loss.
And loss had already moved on without me.

I stand up slowly.

"You shouldn't come here I whisper — mostly to myself.
Not because it was a bad ideal.
Because it's empty.

"I thought I was chasing hope."

I look at the house one last time.

"I was chasing something that had already decided to forget me."

I step off the porch.

"Quietly saying."

"I have to find my mom I have to find my mom."

But this time…
I don't feel strongly about finding her.
It sounds like something you say when you lost, and you don't know where you're sleeping tonight.
Something you say when you've already burned the bridge behind you.

I didn't turn back toward the foster house.
And I don't know where my mother is.

The street doesn't offer answers.
It just stretches forward.

For a while, I just walk.
No destination.
No plan.
Just legs moving under me because stopping feels worse.

This would be my first night with nowhere to sleep.

I end up at a bus stop not far up the street.
Lucky for me, the night is warm.

I don't eat.
I don't drink.
I just sit there, staring at the streetlights, thinking about where my mother could be.

I still believe once I find her, everything will settle.
Everything will make sense again.

But the night isn't peaceful.
Every sound makes me sit up.
Every car makes me tense.

I worry someone might recognize me — or worse, an officer might ask questions and drag me back into custody.
I worry someone might rob me, hurt me.

When you're young and alone, the world grows teeth.

I drift in and out of sleep like someone floating on rough water.

At sunrise, I walk to the Transit Center — the main bus terminal, the place where everyone crosses paths whether they have a car or not. I think maybe if I stay there long enough, somebody I know will show up. Somebody who can tell me where my mother went.

I sit there for hours, watching people come and go, their lives moving fast while mine stands still.

That's when I see somebody from my old school.
A friend.

We talk a little — just regular stuff. Girls. School. Life.
He doesn't know anything about what I've been going through.
I don't tell him.
Something in me feels safer hiding it.

I ask him if he has a little cash.
He hands me ten dollars without hesitation.

I told him I'll pay him back — even though I didn't know when I'll see him again.

When he got on the bus and it pull away, I finally bought food — nothing big, just the kind of meal kids from the hood know well: a soda, a bag of chips, a Debbie cake. Four dollars. Enough to calm the hunger.

The rest I save.
Just in case.

I stay at the transit center all day. The idea of going back to the foster lady's house lingers in my mind, but my spirit rejects it. I can't make myself turn back. Pride, pain, and hope tangle together inside me.

I wait.
I watch the crowd.
I pray silently that someone familiar will pass by.

And then he does.

A familiar face.
A strong face.

My uncle.

I jump up and rush toward him.

"Unk! Unk! Wait — it's me."

He pauses, looking at me like he must remind himself who I am. Maybe life wore him down too. Maybe he didn't expect to see me there like that.

We talk.
I ask him where my mother is.
Why did everyone leave the blue house without telling me?

He said he moved out a while ago.
Tells me my mom is staying on the southside with my Aunt Tonya.

Tells me I should go see my grandfather take bus 10 get off at the last stop I will see the yellow house my grandfather lives in from the bus stop — and he'll know more about where my aunt lived and how to get there.

A part of me knows going to my grandfather's house isn't the best idea. Their relationship — my mom and him — has always been rocky. And he can't stand her husband, not even a little. He isn't a gentle man. His name stays in the middle of every argument, every family problem.

But I have no other options.
No home.
No food.
No plan.
And no mother in sight.

So when the bus heading toward his house comes, I get on.

I get off exactly where my uncle told me and walk toward my grandfather's house. He's already on the porch, staring down the road like he's been expecting me.

When I get there, he starts talking immediately.
Questions.
Stories.

Complaints.
Criticism.
Drama.

He speaks about my mom, her husband, the family history — all tangled in bitterness I don't fully understand. He says I need to get a job. Need to "be a man now."

He doesn't say I can't stay.
But he doesn't have to.

I feel it in his tone.
In the pauses between his sentences.
In the fact that he doesn't offer reassurance — just responsibility.

But he does offer food.
And he does let me crash on the couch for the night.

And after the previous night at the bus stop, that couch feels like heaven.

I fall asleep exhausted.
Still lost.
Still searching.

But warm — for the first time in days

ON THE MOVE

I woke up before my grandfather did.
No alarm.
No noise.
Just that instinct you get when you're somewhere you don't belong — a place when staying too long means hearing too much, feeling too much, or being told things you're too tired to absorb.

The house was quiet in a heavy way.
Not peaceful — just old, still, loaded with years of arguments and distance.

There was no cigarette smell.
No footsteps.
No morning routine.
Just the faint hum of the refrigerator and the weight of everything I'd been carrying.

The couch under me felt rough, but it had still been better than the bus stops the night before. I sat up slowly. My body was stiff. My stomach was empty. My mind was somewhere between exhaustion and survival.

It was around 8 a.m.
Light slipped through the blinds in thin lines, cutting across the floor.
I stood carefully, trying not to creak the old wood. I didn't want to wake him.

Truth?
I didn't want to hear anything else.
Not more talks about my mother.
Not more lectures about being a man.
Not more family drama I was too young and too tired to understand.

I needed to move.
I needed to keep going.
I needed to find my mother.

As I walked toward the door, I paused for half a second — not out of guilt, but out of habit. Wondering if he'd call out. Wondering if he'd say something father-like, something that made me feel seen.

But he didn't.
Still… I knew he heard me.
He wasn't fully asleep.
He knew I was leaving.
He just didn't stop me.

So I opened the door quietly, stepped outside, and let it shut behind me.

The morning air hit my face — cool and honest.
I didn't look back.
I just started walking, hungry, tired, and determined.

I didn't have an address.
I didn't have directions.
I didn't have comfort or guidance.
All I had was the need to find my mother.
And being alone didn't change that.

As I walked up the street away from my grandfather's house, something hit me hard — not just the heat or the hunger, but myself.

I hadn't asked for directions.
I hadn't asked how to get to my aunt's house.
I hadn't asked for the address.
I was so focused on leaving — on escaping his words — that I didn't even get the information I needed.

Three days.
Same clothes.
Same shoes.
No shower.
No toothbrush.
No nothing.

The musk under my arms was strong.
My shirt felt sticky.
My teeth felt gritty.
Even my breath tasted stale.

I looked down at myself as I walked and felt that mix of embarrassment and survival — the quiet understanding that even in my condition, I didn't have time to stop and care.

All I had was seven dollars.
And I already knew I needed $1.25 for the bus fare just to get back to the Transit Center, where all routes connected.
That one ride meant everything.

So I walked to the nearest bus stop the one up the street from my grandfather house and waited.

When the bus pulled up, I stepped on, dropped my fare, and spoke straight to the driver.

"Excuse me… how do I get to the southside?" I asked.

He looked at me — not with pity, but with that calm bus-driver patience.

"Where on the southside?" he asked.

"I'm trying to get to my aunt's house," I said. "I don't know the street… but I know it's near the Food Lion on the southside. The old one."

He nodded, like that was enough.

"Alright. Take this bus to the Transit Center. Then transfer to the 16 or the 12. Both head that way. Tell the next driver what you told me."

I thanked him and went to sit near the back.

The bus pulled off, brakes sighing loud.
The doors folded shut.
The engine hummed.
The city started sliding past the windows.

My head leaned against the bus window.
Eyes heavy.
Body tired in that way life makes you tired — not from running, but from carrying.

Streetlights passed in soft flashes across my face.
Buildings blurred.

The driver spoke again, quieter this time, to someone near the front.

"He's worn out," he said.
"Needs rest… real rest.
Kids like him… we see 'them every day.
Some are running to a home.
Some are running from one.
And the world acts like it's normal."

The bus slowed.

"This is y'all's stop," he said.

A passenger tapped my shoulder gently.
I opened my eyes.
I stood.
I stepped off the bus.

The bus pulled away behind me, its engine fading into the distance, and for a moment the city felt too big and too loud.

This was the Transit Center — the place the first driver told me to reach before switching routes.

I stood there trying not to look as tired as I felt.

Three days in the same clothes.
Three days without real sleep.
Three days without a shower or a real meal.

But I still had to keep going.

I watched people come and go while I waited for the next bus.
I stayed quiet.
Stayed focused.
Held onto the little money I had left.

When the southside bus arrived, I stepped on and looked at that driver the same way.

"Southside?" I asked.

"Yeah," he said. "I'll tell you when to get off."

I nodded and took a seat by the window.

The bus rolled deeper into a part of town where the buildings changed, the people changed, the roads changed.

But one thing stayed the same inside me:

I needed to find my mother.
No matter how I smelled,
no matter how hungry I was,
no matter how lost I felt…

I kept going.
Because stopping wasn't an option.

SOUTHSIDE

When the bus slowed near the gas station across from the old Food Lion, the driver looked at me through the mirror and said, "This your stop."

No advice.

No warning.

Just that.

I stepped off the bus and felt the heat hit me like it had been waiting.

The southside had a different kind of air — heavier, louder, watching everything. The Food Lion looked tired, the parking lot cracked, and the gas station next to it felt like it had lived through more fights than customers.

This wasn't a place to be lost.

But lost was all I was.

I walked into the gas station with the little money I had left. The clerk locked onto me the second the door beeped. He stared at me like he had already decided I was trouble — no mercy, no curiosity, just suspicion.

I grabbed what I always grabbed:

A soda.

A bag of chips.

A Debbie cake.

Survival.

When I put the items on the counter, he asked,

"Find everything okay?"

But his tone meant something completely different:

I'm watching you. Don't try anything.

"Yes," I said.

He bagged my snacks slowly, eyes never leaving me.

I took the black plastic bag and stepped outside.

And that's when I saw the road I had to walk.

A long, empty stretch of asphalt.

No houses.

No trees.
No sidewalks.
Just heat, dirt, and silence.
To my right stood one beat-up apartment complex — balconies fading, paint peeling. After that, nothing but open road.
I started walking.
My shoes crunched gravel along the edge because there wasn't a sidewalk. Dust kicked up around my ankles. Cars passed slowly, like they needed time to study me. Windows half-down. Eyes staring from the shade.
The sun sat straight over my head, pressing on my neck and shoulders. Sweat rolled down my back, sticking my shirt to my skin. My clothes smelled like three days without a shower. My teeth felt gritty. My mouth was dry.
But I kept going.
Fifteen minutes.
One long road.
Nothing but heat and memories that weren't even clear — just faint pieces of childhood from when my mother first lived here.
A left turn we used to take.
A little hill we'd race down.
A street where we'd split ten dollars five ways to buy snacks from this same store.
Those memories — small as they were — guided me like weak street signs.
When I reached the four-way intersection, I crossed and kept walking another long stretch.
And finally, the neighborhood appeared.
Porches.
Kids.
Voices.
Laughter.
Life.
It felt like stepping into a different world after that empty road. Kids were running, yelling, playing. People sat outside talking loudly. Cars rattled over speed bumps.

Then I heard something familiar —
A voice.
A laugh.
Something that pulled at a memory inside me.
I followed it.
And then I saw him.
My cousin.
The same cousin I used to walk these same streets with.
The same one I used to race down hills with.
The same one I spent those ten-dollar snack runs with.
Hope hit my chest so hard I almost forgot I was tired.
I walked faster.
"Cuzzo!" I called out.
He turned quick, eyes wide, then smiled hard and walked toward me.
"Idress! Man, where you been?" he said, dapping me up strong, gripping my hand like family does when they're genuinely happy to see you.
He looked at me closely —
Not judging.
But seeing.
Seeing the sweat.
The exhaustion.
The clothes I hadn't changed in days.
Seeing the pain I was trying to hide.
We talked for a few minutes —
Just catching up.
Talking about the block.
Talking about nothing and everything at the same time.
Then, out of nowhere, like it was nothing, he said,
"Yo, your mom at my house."
Everything inside me stopped.
The heat.
The noise.
The exhaustion.
All of it froze for half a second.

I swallowed hard.

"Which house?" I asked.

He pointed down the street.

"Right there — third one on the left."

I nodded slowly, holding in a breath I didn't realize I had trapped inside me.

"Good looking out, cuz," I said quietly.

He dapped me up again, gripping my hand tight, like he understood how much this moment meant.

I turned toward the direction he pointed.

And for the first time in days —

After sleeping outside,

After walking miles in the heat,

After searching without answers,

After feeling invisible —

I felt like I was walking toward something.

Toward someone.

Toward home — or whatever pieces of it were left.

Then I took my first step toward the house where my mother was staying.

NO PLACE FOR ME

My aunt's house looked quiet from the outside, but when I stepped onto the porch, I could already hear the life inside — music somewhere in the back, a TV too loud, voices overlapping. Before I knocked, I hesitated.

That knock felt heavy.

It felt like whatever answered on the other side would determine everything.

I stood there in the heat — three days in the same clothes, sweat on my skin, stomach empty, mind exhausted. My hand hovered over the door because I feared the answer.

Would they let me stay?

Would I even be welcome?

Was this finally a place to rest… or another door closing?

I finally knocked.

Soft.

Then louder.

The door opened, and my aunt's face appeared. When she saw me, her expression softened — relief and worry mixed.

"Hey, baby," she said, pulling me in for a quick hug. "Your mama in the back."

I stepped inside.

The air hit me immediately — thick with the smell of weed. The house wasn't filthy, but it wasn't clean either. Shoes in the corner. Clothes on a chair. Curtains half hanging. The AC hummed weakly, blowing more warm air than cold.

It felt crowded. Lived in. Tense.

But it was still family.

I walked down the hallway toward my mother's room.

Before I could knock, the door opened.

Her husband stepped out.

The second he saw me, he froze — like he didn't expect my body to be standing in this doorway, in this new house, at this moment.

"I… I didn't know you was here," he said.

He didn't mean he didn't know I was released.

He meant he didn't know I would show up here.
His eyes stayed wide as he tried to explain.
"We moved a little while back. Your mama been real sick. Things been rough. We thought you was staying where you were… everything just happened quick."
I didn't respond.
Didn't explain.
Didn't tell him I slept outside, walked miles, went days without showering.
I just stepped past him.
Because I needed to see her.
My mother.
She lay in the bed, still and quiet, her body small under the blanket.
She looked weak — not tired, but sick in a way that made my chest tighten.
"Hey, Mama," I said softly.
She turned her head slowly, like every movement cost her strength she didn't have.
"I love you," she whispered.
That was all she had energy for.
Those three soft words.
She didn't ask where I'd been.
Didn't ask if I had eaten.
Didn't ask where I was sleeping that night.
Maybe she already knew.
Maybe she didn't have the energy to ask questions she couldn't fix.
I sat with her for a moment, feeling everything — love, fear, sadness, confusion, and a weight I couldn't name.
"I'll be right back," I told her.
She nodded faintly.
I stepped out and walked to the living room where my aunt was.
"Can I stay here tonight?" I asked softly.
Her answer came fast.
Not harsh — just honest.
"No, Idress… we don't have the room."
The words hit like a stone dropping into my chest.

I didn't say anything back.
Didn't argue.
Didn't get angry.
I just swallowed the pain.
I didn't go tell my mother.
I wouldn't do that to her — not when she was lying in someone else's house, sick, barely hanging on.
I walked back into her room one last time.
"Ma… it's getting late. I got to go."
Her eyes lifted slowly.
"Where are you staying?" she whispered.
I had no answer.
None I could say without breaking her.
"I'll be back," I said instead.
Her husband walked back inside, and I stepped out of the room.
When I reached the front door, he called out.
"Idress."
I turned.
He walked closer, rubbing the back of his neck like he wasn't sure how to say it.
"You remember Dave?" he asked.
I nodded.
"Light-skin Dave? From the blue house?"
That was all I said out loud.
But in my head, memories came —
The pills.
The weed.
The drinking.
How he supplied her husband sometimes.
I didn't speak those things.
Just kept them inside.
"I'll call him," he said.
He went to the back room to make the call, leaving me standing near the door.
Five minutes passed.
He came back out.

"Dave said meet him at the gas station up the street. He said he'll take you in for tonight. Y'all talk more in the morning."

It made sense.

Dave didn't live right there —

he lived about a ten-minute drive away.

Close enough to help.

Far enough that I couldn't walk.

The gas station was the easiest meeting point for both of us.

I nodded slowly.

It wasn't home.

It wasn't comfort.

But it was the only place I could go.

I stepped outside and started walking back up the hill.

Halfway up, my cousin saw me again.

"You are heading out, cuzzo?"

"Yeah," I said.

And kept walking.

Toward the gas station.

Toward Dave.

Toward whatever the night had for me.

That was when it hit me the hardest:

You can knock on family's door…

and still have no place for yourself.

DAVE

Walking back toward the gas station that night — hungry, tired, clothes sticking to my skin — one thought stayed in my head through all the confusion:

I was only a few weeks away from turning sixteen.

Still fifteen.

Still a kid.

Still trying to survive day by day with no direction, no home, no plan.

When I reached the top of the hill, I saw a silver Chevy Malibu parked under a streetlight, engine running low.

Inside sat Dave.

Light-skinned.

Goatee.

Long hair tied up in that loose top ponytail he never fixed.

A cigarette resting between two fingers.

Styles P / D-Block humming low through the speakers.

Dave looked at me once — that older New York head-nod type glance — and said,

"Ayo… get in."

Calm.

Short.

No questions.

I opened the door and sat down.

The seats were cloth, warm, worn in.

The car smelled like smoke, weed, and long nights.

Dave pulled off quietly.

After a minute, he asked,

"You hungry?"

"Yeah."

He nodded.

We pulled into McDonald's. He leaned his head slightly and asked,

"What you want?"

Not rude.
Not soft.
Just a grown New York man speaking straight.
I told him.
He ordered.
Paid.
Took the bag from the worker.
Then handed it to me.
He didn't tell me to eat.
Didn't comment.
Didn't question anything.
He just let me eat.
I tore into the food fast, starving, lost in each bite. Dave didn't look at me or make it weird — he kept driving slowly while Styles P talked pain, survival, and street truths through the speakers.
Ten minutes later, he turned into a place I never expected:
A gated apartment community.
Tall metal gate.
Security keypad.
Clean sidewalks.
Quiet air that didn't match anything I came from.
Dave typed a code.
The gate opened.
"We in the back," he said.
We parked.
The wooden stairs going up were clean and sturdy.
"We up top."
We walked to the third floor. Dave flicked his cigarette off the balcony rail with that smooth older-New York flick.
Then he unlocked the door.
As soon as it opened, a black female pitbull shot forward, barking loud, tail wagging like she'd been waiting on somebody.
Dave put his hand down, calm.
"Ayo… chill, mama. She doesn't bite, B."
She ran straight at me — circling, sniffing, nudging my leg with her nose.

Dave nodded.

"Friendly."

Inside felt different than any place I'd been in a long time.

Quiet.

Still.

Safe.

Dave pointed to the room on the right.

"Aight… that's your room right there.

No extra talking.

No instructions.

Just the space, the tone, and his trust — in his own way.

Inside the room was:

A mattress on a box spring

Brownish-white carpet

A closet with some boxes

My own bathroom

A window facing the gate

It wasn't much.

But it was more than I had anywhere else.

The sun woke me early.

When I stepped into the main area, I saw the apartment clearly for the first time.

The living room had:

One couch

A TV on a stand

The PS3 next to it, controllers lined up, Dynasty Warriors case right beside it

That was where Dave chilled — smoking, gaming, unwinding, thinking.

Against the wall between the kitchen and my room was the computer.

But that wasn't Dave's spot.

That was Nene's spot.

Her computer.

Her desk.

Her little corner of the apartment.

The kitchen was modern:
Updated appliances
Clean counters
No barstools
There was a balcony off the living room with the door cracked, letting in cool air.
The pitbull — Smoke — ran up again, tail moving like she'd known me forever.
Dave was already up.
Hair half slipping out the ponytail, cigarette burning slow.
He said,
"Ayo… take that trash out. Then walk Smoke."
I did both.
Walking through that gated community felt unreal — quiet, safe, steady.
When I came back inside, Nene walked through grabbing her bag.
"Morning," she said.
"Morning."
Dave grabbed his keys — same routine every morning.
Nene didn't drive. No license.
Dave drove her everywhere.
"Aight, come on," he told her.
When Dave returned, he went straight to the kitchen cabinet, reached up, grabbed a bottle, and poured one shot of liquor.
He drank it quiet.
Then he sat on the couch with his cigarette and looked at me steady.
"Aight… what's your plan?"
"I don't have one. Am not in school. Am not working."
Dave nodded slowly — older, calm, firm.
"Look, B… you can stay. But you not sitting' in this apartment all day. You got to be doing' something. School or work. Something'."
Then he laid out the rules — real OG tone:
"Ayo… listen.

and nobody coming' in this apartment but you.
No friends. None."
He pointed toward the door with his chin.
"If somebody giving' you a ride, you get dropped off up the street.
You get picked up the street.
I don't need nobody knowing' where I live."
Then:
"And no drugs. No alcohol. Not in here."
He didn't raise his voice.
Didn't repeat himself.
His eyes said everything.
What Dave Never Showed Me
One thing I figured out fast —
Dave never exposed me to none of the street side of his life.
I knew he was connected.
I knew he knew my uncles.
I knew he knew my mom's husband.
I knew the type of world they came from.
But with me?
He never brought anybody around.
He never talked business near me.
He never made street calls in front of me.
He never moved anything inside the apartment.
He never put me in anything.
He kept that world far from where I slept.
Protected me from it in his own quiet way.
I stayed with Dave long enough to watch my life shift.
I turned sixteen in that apartment — just a few weeks after he picked me up from the gas station.
A year later, I turned seventeen there too.
Two birthdays.
Two years.
Two versions of myself.
And through every lie, every disappearance, every moment where family vanished on me again
Dave stayed solid.

He gave me:
Food
Clothes
Structure
Space
Safety
Rules
Honesty
A place to breathe
He wasn't my father.
But he was the first man
who stayed long enough
for me to grow up under the same roof as him.
After a while, calling him "Dave" didn't fit anymore.
I started calling him:
Uncle Dave.
Because by then…
that's exactly who he was.

THE QUIET YEAR

My first year living with Dave was the quietest year of my whole teenage life.
No chaos.
No explosions.
No surprises waiting around corners.
Just the same soft rhythm, day after day — something I wasn't used to.
When I moved into that apartment, I was only a few weeks away from turning sixteen.
Still fifteen.
Still carrying everything I'd been through.
Still trying to figure out why life kept dropping me into empty spaces.
But nothing about that year felt empty.
It was… steady.
Dave didn't pressure me.
After that first conversation about school or work, he never brought it up again.
Never asked me where I was going during the day.
Never asked what I planned to do with my life.
Sometimes he mentioned my mom — quick, almost offhand.
"Ayo, your moms husband owes me money."
Whatever that meant, he left it alone.
Never asked me about her again.
Never pushed for details.
Never used my situation to guilt me or make me feel like a burden.
He just let me be.
Some mornings, Dave tapped the wall or called out:
"Ayo, come on, ride with us."
And I'd jump in the car while he drove Nene to work.
Smoke — the pitbull — would pace around excited, trying to run out the door with us.

Dave would smoke his cigarette with the window cracked, D-Block playing low, Nene talking about her shift or something somebody said at her job.

The way they moved together felt… normal.

Like a real couple.

A real home.

A real life.

Sometimes Nene cooked for me.

Simple meals — rice, chicken, pasta — but they felt like more than food.

She'd joke around, laugh loud, talk to me like I wasn't some lost kid who landed on their doorstep.

It felt human.

It felt warm.

Sometimes Dave let me ride along when he ran errands. Or if I was out walking somewhere close, he'd pull up slow and say,

"Ayo, hop in."

No questions.

No lectures.

Just a ride.

Eventually, he put me on his phone line.

Just handed me the phone one day and said,

"Keep that on. In case I call you."

Like it was nothing.

But it wasn't nothing.

It was connection.

It was someone reaching out instead of walking away.

He gave me small cash sometimes too.

Not a lot.

Just enough for bus rides and something to eat.

Everything was simple.

Everything felt… okay.

I can't remember a single moment he was ever mad at me.

Not once.

It felt like he wanted good for me — even if he wasn't the type to say that out loud.

Even if he didn't know how to show it in the usual ways.
Time moved slow but steady.
Days slid into weeks.
Weeks turned into months.
And somewhere in that stillness, somewhere in that quiet routine…
I turned sixteen.
Sixteen in that same room with the mattress on the box spring and the brownish carpet.
Sixteen in a place where nobody yelled.
Nobody disappeared.
Nobody woke me up with chaos.
And then, before I knew it, the seasons changed again, and I turned seventeen in that same apartment.
Seventeen waking up to sunlight instead of worry.
Seventeen walking Smoke in the mornings.
Seventeen taking out trash, catching buses, wandering the city without fear the day would destroy me.
Seventeen watching Dave and Nene move around the apartment like a small, quiet family I somehow found myself inside of.
For the first time in years, I had peace.
Not happiness — not yet — but peace.
A roof.
A routine.
A place to breathe.
That summer, at seventeen…
I met the mother of my first child.
And just like that, the quiet year ended,
and a new chapter of my life began.

THE UNEXPECTED BEGINNING

I met Vic at a bus stop on a random day.

Two teenagers waiting on a late bus, talking about the girls walking by, laughing like we'd known each other longer than ten minutes.

Before the bus came, he asked, "Bro, you hoop?"

I said yeah.

He told me the courts were down the street and to hit him later.

We exchanged numbers.

That was the start.

Our apartment complexes sat next to each other — his worn-down and loud, mine a little cleaner but still the hood.

Some days we walked to the court together. Other days, one of us was already there warming up.

It was at those courts — and at the pond behind his complex — that everything shifted.

The pond was peaceful.

Ducks gliding across the water.

Evening sun dropping low.

The whole area quiet except for kids running around or a couple arguing in the distance.

That's where Vic introduced me to her.

She was there with him — his girl at the time.

Brown skin.

Big eyes.

A smile you couldn't forget.

Slim frame.

Goofy, playful, easy to talk to.

Soft energy.

I didn't say much the first few times.

I was the third wheel — the friend tagging along, throwing rocks in the water, feeding ducks with them, laughing but staying in the background.

Still…

something about her stayed with me.

Vic used to tease her, calling her by her first and last name like a joke. He said it so much I memorized it without trying.
That detail became important later.
We hung at that pond a few times — just kids killing time, enjoying simple evenings.
Then one day, Vic told me they broke up.
He said it casually.
Didn't think twice.
But it stayed in my mind.
The next time I had access to Nene's computer, I searched her name on MySpace — back when everyone used real names.
I stared at her profile picture longer than I should've, hoping she would remember me.
I sent her a message.
Simple.
Nothing crazy.
She replied.
We talked.
One message turned into ten.
Ten turned into hours.
Hours turned into something deeper.
Eventually, I asked if she wanted to see me.
We met at the front gate of my complex at first.
I still followed Dave's rules — nobody inside.
She showed up in a car; I didn't know whose.
She always came in the late afternoon, stayed an hour or two, then left before it got dark.
As days passed, she came more often.
The attachment grew fast.
We couldn't stay away from each other.
Soon, I started sneaking her into Dave and Nene's apartment.
By then, I had a key.
I'd pretend I was leaving for the day, wait until they pulled off, then text her to come through.
We were teenagers doing what teenagers do — not always innocent but always trying to hold onto the hours we had.

One day Dave caught us walking out.
He didn't blow up.
He didn't yell.
He just gave me that older New York look like, "Aight, so you are doing your thing, huh?"
He didn't mind.
But Nene laid the rules.
No crazy drama.
No pregnancy talk.
No bringing stress into their home.
No playing house like we grown.
We agreed.
Even though the connection between us was already deeper than anyone realized.
After that, she didn't have to sneak anymore.
She started coming over freely.
Talking to me.
Laughing with me.
Being there.
The truth is…
she became the first person who saw something in me when I didn't see it in myself.
Everywhere we went, she pushed me forward.
She believed in me.
She looked at me like I had value.
Like I had a chance to be something.
I didn't know it then,
but this girl — the girl from the pond —
would become the one who changed my entire life.
And none of it was planned.
It was…
The Unexpected Beginning.

THE TRUTH THAT BROKE THE QUITE

Everything between me and her felt calm at first.
Not perfect.
Not planned.
But calm.
The late-night talks.
The sneaking around.
The laughter in Dave's living room.
The closeness that kept pulling us toward each other.
It all created this quiet space in my life — a space where nothing hurt, nothing chased me, nothing felt dangerous.
For the first time, I had peace.
But peace doesn't last forever.
Not when you're young.
Not when you're figuring things out without guidance.
Not when feelings turn into actions, and actions turn into consequences.
It started with her acting different.
Not distant — just off. Quiet.
Her messages felt heavier. Her smile looked forced. She'd sit beside me at Dave's house, close enough to touch, but I could tell she wasn't fully there. Something was swirling in her mind.
One afternoon she looked at me and said,
"I got to tell you something."
Five words that shift the ground under your feet.
She took a breath, looked down, and said it straight.
"I think I'm pregnant."
The room went quiet.
The kind of quiet that isn't peaceful.
The kind that presses against your chest.
My heart dropped.
My hands got cold.

Everything inside me started moving fast and slow at the same time.
I wasn't ready.
I didn't understand the weight.
I was only a teenager — still half child, half trying to figure out life.
No job.
No steady school.
No real guidance.
Just a girl I cared about and a future I didn't see coming.
But she wasn't lying.
She wasn't guessing.
A few days later, she showed me the test.
Positive.
That moment split my life into two halves —
Before I knew.
And after I knew.
I didn't know what to say.
I didn't know what came next.
I didn't know how to be a father when I barely knew how to be myself.
But I knew one thing:
I couldn't hide this forever.
And the place I lived — Dave's place — wasn't just four walls and a couch to crash on.
They cared.
They guided.
They stepped up when nobody else did.
They deserved the truth.
And I knew that truth was going to hit their peace like a stone through glass.
The day I decided to tell them, everything in my chest felt tight.
I waited until Dave and Nene were both home — the worst timing, the only timing.
The apartment felt smaller than usual.
Every sound louder.
Every breath heavier.

Nene was in the kitchen.
Dave was in the living room playing a game on the PS3, like nothing in the world was wrong.
But inside me?
Everything felt wrong.
I stood there trying to find the words.
Trying not to let my voice shake.
Trying to prepare myself for disappointment, anger, confusion — whatever was coming.
Finally, I said it.
"Nene… Dave… I need to tell y'all something."
Both looked at me.
Not angry.
Just waiting.
And I felt myself slipping out of childhood right there.
I swallowed hard and said,
"She's pregnant."
The words cracked the quiet open like thunder.
Nene's expression changed first — not anger, not shock, but something deeper. A mix of worry and reality settling in all at once.
Dave paused the game and leaned back slowly, rubbing his chin, eyes locked on me.
Nobody yelled.
Nobody cursed.
Nobody told me to get out.
But the silence that followed…
That silence was heavier than any yelling could've been.
I stood there feeling everything at once —
Fear.
Shame.
Guilt.
Responsibility.
Confusion.
Like I had done something I couldn't undo.
Like I was standing at the edge of a future I wasn't ready for.

Nene finally spoke.
Her voice wasn't loud.
It was steady.
Serious.
Cutting.
"Do you understand what this means?"
I nodded.
But I didn't.
Not fully.
Not yet.
Dave exhaled through his nose, stood up, walked past me once, then came back and sat down.
He didn't look angry.
Just older.
Maybe tired.
"Alright," he said quietly.
"Then we do what we got to do."
No lectures.
No threats.
Just reality.
And in that moment, I realized something:
Childhood doesn't leave you gently.
It doesn't slip away or fade out.
It breaks.
It cracks.
It shatters when the truth gets too heavy to hold.
And that day —
Standing in front of the only two adults who ever truly looked out for me —
I felt it break.

SACRIFICES

After the truth came out, Dave's apartment didn't feel the same.

Not in a bad way — just heavier.

Like everybody in that space understood life had shifted, and nothing was going back to how it was. The late-night sneaking, the quiet moments, the young love — all of it felt different with a baby on the way.

I didn't know how to be a father.

I barely knew how to be steady.

But I already understood something big:

Being young wasn't an excuse anymore.

Everything I did next wasn't just about me.

It was about the life coming into the world.

That's where the sacrifice began.

The Social Security Office

The first thing I needed was my Social Security card.

But getting it wasn't simple for someone like me.

We had to go in person, and the whole ride there, I felt this tight fear in my chest. I didn't know if CPS would still have my name in the system — if someone could pull up a file and say I wasn't supposed to be walking around free. I kept imagining someone calling the police. Someone recognizing my situation.

I was still considered a runaway.

I didn't want to get locked up again.

But she stayed by my side through all of it.

She was supposed to be in school, or with her family, or anywhere else — but she chose to help me. She understood a world I didn't, and she knew how to move through it.

We waited in line almost an hour.

People arguing.

Kids whining.

Numbers being called over the intercom.

I kept looking over my shoulder like trouble was coming for me.

When we finally reached the window, the lady behind the glass asked for ID.

I didn't have one — that was the whole point.

All I had was the community college transcript with my picture on it. The address printed on it wasn't even right.

Honestly, I don't think we had half the paperwork we were supposed to have.

The worker looked at me.

Then she looked at her — the girl helping me stand up straighter in life.

And without any questions or trouble, she just said:

"It's ten dollars for the mailing fee."

That was it.

No issues.

No roadblocks.

No "come back later."

No "you're missing this."

No calling anyone.

She paid the fee.

We left.

And a few weeks later, the card came to Dave's apartment — the first piece of official paperwork with my name on it that felt like mine.

I called her immediately.

"I got it," I said, excitement running through me.

Because this meant I could finally apply for an ID.

And an ID meant a job.

And a job meant I was stepping into something real.

She was happy for me — genuinely happy — and it made me feel seen in a way I never had before.

The DMV

A few days later, we went to the DMV.

The line was long. The sun was hot, beating down on everybody waiting outside.

She stood beside me looking simple and beautiful:

Blue jeans.

Tennis shoes.

A white shirt.

That soft perfume she always wore.
Hair pulled back in a ponytail.
She looked like peace in a place full of frustration.
We stood there knowing this was the day I wouldn't be invisible anymore.
This was the day I finally got something with my name on it — something the world had to recognize.
I was nervous.
Excited.
My heart was racing.
As the line moved, I don't know what came over me, but I reached out and held her hand.
She looked down at our hands, then at me.
She didn't let go.
We moved up slowly, step by step, until we reached the door.
Inside, they checked my documents.
Typed my information.
Then told me to stand in front of the camera.
This was the first picture of my life that wasn't taken inside a jail.
Not a mugshot.
Not a record.
A picture of freedom.
A picture of progress.
A picture of a boy stepping into manhood because life forced him to rise.
They snapped it.
We paid the fee.
And when we got back to the car, I hugged her.
Not a quick hug — a real one.
I held my tears back.
She hugged me like she understood everything I couldn't say.
And Dave and Nene were watching everything quietly.
Dave and Nene checked on everything I was doing.
Not in a controlling way — in a concerned way.
I couldn't tell if they wanted me out soon or if they were just making sure, I stayed on track. They never said they wanted me

gone. They never made me feel unwelcome. But they were watching me closely, making sure I took the right steps.
Me and her became their concern too.
They saw the pregnancy.
They saw her helping me.
They saw she had things I didn't — a car, a stable family, education, support.
I think they expected her to help guide me.
And she did.
Between her, Dave, and Nene —
I finally had direction.
That's what sacrifice was for me:
Giving up the version of myself that wouldn't survive the future I was walking into.
Letting go of the boy who hid, who ran, who didn't understand anything.
Becoming someone who could stand up for the life he created.
Whether I was ready or not,
I was stepping into manhood.

THE TEST

I met her parents for the first time at my apartment complex.

It wasn't the whole family — just her, her mother, and her father.

She walked a little ahead of them, nervous in her smile, like she wanted this moment to matter. Like she hoped her parents would see something in me she already saw.

Her father stepped forward first.

He was shorter than wife — about 5'6, stocky, solid. The kind of man who didn't need height to have authority. His skin was in-between — not light, not dark — with the voice and posture of someone who had worked with his hands his whole life.

Her mother stood beside him, taller than he was, the same height as their daughter. Similar features, but her mother carried a sharp, protective energy — the kind of woman who evaluates you the second she sees you.

And then there was her —

Taller than her father.

Standing next to me.

Hoping this meeting would go right.

We talked a little.

Small things.

Respectful things.

Nothing deep.

But even without depth, I felt the truth:

They didn't trust me.

They didn't understand me.

They didn't see me as someone ready for their daughter.

Still, the introduction happened.

And that was the beginning.

The Cleaning Job — The Real Test

About a week later, she called me.

"My dad asked if you want to help clean a building with us," she said.

"We're all going."

She didn't say it was a test.

She didn't say it meant anything more.

So I went.

The next day, they picked me up — the whole family squeezed into the car. Her father driving. Her mother in the front. Her and her brothers in the back. And me slipping in among them, the outsider stepping into a family space for the first time.

When we got to the building, everything moved fast.

Her father passed out the cleaning supplies — mops, buckets, rags. No instructions. Everyone already knew what to do. This was their rhythm. Their routine.

I joined in.

Trying to keep up.

Trying to show effort.

Trying to show I wasn't lazy or helpless.

It didn't take long to understand what was really happening:

This wasn't just work.

This was the silent test.

Her father didn't speak to me directly, but he talked while we cleaned — loud enough for me to hear, calm enough to pretend it wasn't about me.

He talked about:

- Being responsible
- Providing
- Being a real man
- Standing on your own
- Having something to offer a woman
- Not depending on anybody

He never had to look at me.

His words already landed where he wanted them to.

And I understood what he saw:

A boy with nothing.

No stable home.

No car.

No money.

No family structure.

No guaranteed future.

And a baby on the way.
I left that building knowing exactly where I stood.
In his eyes —
I wasn't enough.
And that was the beginning of the pressure.

Her World vs. Mine

The more we talked, the more I learned how different she grew up.
Five brothers.
One roof.
Loud but loyal.
Structure.
Rules.
Meals at the table.
Expectations.
She had a mother and father who stayed.
She started community college.
She kept moving forward.
Meanwhile, my life felt like it was moving in circles — stops, starts, temporary progress.
We came from two different worlds.

Dave and Nene Move to the West Side

Around that time, Dave and Nene told me they were moving.
Rent was too high. They wanted to save up and buy a house.
So we moved to the west side —
Closer to my grandfather.
Cheaper.
Rougher.
Louder.
Not as safe.
But it changed one thing that mattered in that moment:
She could come over more.
Her school was close by.
She didn't need her car to see me.
Because I could go see her the bus went straight to her school.
Her parents hated that.

They didn't want her near me.
They didn't want her coming around.
They started taking her car away.
Started controlling her movements.
Started tightening everything around her.
But she still came.
Often enough that it felt like she lived with us.
Dave and Nene noticed.
They weren't dumb.
So one day, they sat me down.
"You're working now.
You got a girl coming over every day.
And you about to be a father.
It's time for you to pay a bill."
This wasn't optional.
This wasn't a suggestion.
This was responsibility.
They were telling me:
If you're going to live here,
If you're going to have her here,
If you're going to be a father —
You need to contribute.
And I respected it.
I needed that guidance.
It was the first real lesson in manhood I ever received.
Her Instability Begins
But things at her own home were falling apart.
The tension with her parents got too heavy, and she couldn't stay there anymore.
She began bouncing between relatives:
Her grandmother Darling.
Her aunt Cindy.
Back and forth.
Cindy was the one I saw most.
Mid-light skin.
Dreads.

Glasses.

A little chunky.

Chill, understanding energy.

Married. No kids.

A dog that barked nonstop.

She didn't let me spend the night.

But she let my girl stay.

Let her use her car.

Let her breathe.

Her home became our closest thing to stability.

But watching her be pushed out of her own house because of me

That hurts.

It made me angry.

Confused.

Guilty.

I kept asking myself:

Why couldn't her parents just get to know me?

Why judge me without understanding me?

Why did she have to suffer because of my situation?

Those questions followed me everywhere.

Leaving Dave and Nene Without a Word

Then I made one of the hardest mistakes of my life.

As her pregnancy moved forward, she was staying at Cindy's — way across town.

An hour by bus.

Twenty minutes by car.

I felt wrong staying at Dave and Nene's while she was so far.

I felt like I was taking advantage.

And I didn't know how to ask if she could stay with us.

I feared the answer.

So one day after work…

I didn't go back.

No goodbye.

No explanation.

Just gone.

I quit McDonald's around the same time.

Life slipped apart again.
And that guilt hit me hard —
Because they had taken me in.
Gave me structure.
Gave me a home.
And I walked away quietly.
It still sits with me.
Back Into Survival Mode
After leaving, I stayed wherever I could.
Cindy's house during the day.
My aunt's sometimes.
Bus stops.
Walking everywhere.
Nowhere stable.
I got a job at Taco Bell on the far side of the city — third shift.
Not because I wanted nights.
But because nights meant shelter.
I worked seven days a week. No days off.
Not working —
Surviving.
Long bus rides.
Heavy nights.
Early mornings.
All for a child that wasn't here yet but was already changing my life.
Every day felt like a test.
A test of strength.
A test of direction.
A test of who I was becoming.
And step by step,
shift by shift,
I kept going —
Toward the moment my son would enter this world
and everything would shift again.

BECOMING THE FATHER I NEVER HAD

I wasn't with her when she went into labor.
I was at Taco Bell, working my overnight shift — tired, hungry, surviving the only way I knew how.
The night felt like every other night until my phone buzzed in my pocket.
When I answered, I heard her breathing hard. Her voice shaking.
"Idress… I think I'm about to have the baby… I'm headed to the hospital…"
I could hear the pain.
The tears.
The fear.
And behind her, her aunt yelling, "Come on, let's go!"
Before I could even speak, the call ended.
I clocked out immediately.
Didn't ask.
Didn't explain.
I didn't care if I got fired.
I ran to the bus stop, watching the minutes stretch like hours as I waited.
The bus ride felt endless — forty long minutes of pacing, praying, replaying her voice in my head.
By the time I made it to the hospital, everyone was already there.
Her grandmother.
Her aunt.
Her brothers.
Even people I didn't recognize.
But I was too late.
My son was already born.
I sat in the waiting room, breathing hard from the rush, the fear, the adrenaline still running through me.
Another man was sitting there too — her father.

Stocky.
Silent.
Arms folded.
Eyes full of judgment.
He didn't speak.
He didn't ask how I was.
He didn't congratulate me.
He just looked at me like I didn't belong there.
Like I had no right to show up.
Like I wasn't needed.
I sat there anyway.
Minutes passed slow.
Voices came and went.
And finally, her grandmother and aunt stepped out of the room.
They looked at me with a warmth her parents never gave me.
"Come on," they said. "Your son is here."
Those words hit me harder than anything in my life.
I stepped into the room, and everything went quiet.
My son was lying in the clear hospital bin beside her bed — wrapped tight, small, new, real.
The doctor looked at me.
"Are you the father?"
"Yes."
My son's mother looked at me with a glow that said everything she didn't have to say out loud:
We did it.
He's here.
Our son is here.
I felt happiness, shock, fear, pride — all at once.
A mix I'd never felt before.
I didn't cry.
But something inside me cracked open.
I signed my son's birth certificate.
Put my name on something real.
Something alive.
The first thing in my life that belonged to me.

I stayed until her family slowly left, one by one.
She eventually fell asleep.
My son beside her, wrapped tight in blankets, breathing small.
I stood there staring.
Feeling everything.
Feeling nothing.
I should've stayed.
I should've slept in that chair.
I should've asked where I belonged.
But I didn't know how to exist in that room with her whole family ready to judge me for breathing wrong.
I needed air.
I needed space.
I needed to think.
It was early evening — maybe 8 PM.
Normally, I'd be deep into my shift.
Working the fry station.
Wiping counters.
Lifting heavy boxes.
But that night, I wasn't going back.
I left the hospital.
Not because I wanted to —
but because I didn't know where I fit.
I walked.
And walked.
And walked.
Another night with no place to stay.
Another night in the cold.
Another night being a father without a foundation.
I stayed out all night, wandering the streets, carrying a new name in my chest:
Dad.
A name I had never said before.
A name I never heard from my own father.
A name that felt heavy and holy at the same time.
I didn't sleep.

I didn't eat.
I didn't know where I was going.
All I knew was this:
My son was here.
Life was different now.
And somehow,
I had to become the father I never had.

ADJUSTIONING TO MY REALITIES

The next morning, I went back to the hospital.

My legs were heavy from walking all night — no sleep, no food, no real place to rest.

But none of that mattered when I walked through those hospital doors.

She was sitting up when I came in.

Hair messy.

Eyes tired.

Beautiful in a way only a new mother can be.

My son was in her arms, feeding. Tiny hands curled into fists.

For the first time, it felt real.

It felt good.

It felt like maybe life had finally given me something that was mine.

Her aunt and grandmother came by early that morning to check on us.

They acted normal — smiling, asking how the night went.

Neither one mentioned me not staying.

Maybe they didn't notice.

Maybe they knew I had nowhere to go.

Maybe her aunt understood more than she ever said — she knew about my job, my bus rides, my unstable life.

Her parents didn't return.

Not her father.

Not her mother.

Not her brothers.

Just us.

Just her.

Just our son.

I stayed the whole day — restless, exhausted, but proud.

Watching her hold him.

Feed him.

Whisper to him.

Looking at him lying in the clear newborn bin beside her bed.

I imagined us having our own place.
Our own home.
Somewhere stable.
But reality always hits harder than hope.
We didn't have anything.
No home.
No money saved.
No car.
No support.
She had more than I had — and even she didn't have enough.
Time moved fast.
Before I realized it, the day was gone.
I had to go to work that night, no matter how tired or overwhelmed I was.
I left the hospital and went straight to Taco Bell.
When I walked in, my manager looked at me with concern.
I explained why I ran out the night before.
She nodded.
"I figured something happened. You told me the baby was on the way. I put extra people on the schedule for the next few weeks. Don't worry about last night. Just breathe."
She was a hippie-type woman — free spirit, warm smile, always felt like she floated instead of walked.
Sometimes she'd ask me, "You ready to be a dad?"
I never really knew how to answer.
She knew I took the bus across the city every night.
She knew I worked nights because I had no other option and possibly nowhere to stay.
But she supported me.
Truth is, my son's mother is the one who helped me get that job.
One day we were leaving her grandmother's house — hungry, tired, with nowhere to go.
We passed the Taco Bell and saw a hiring sign in the window.
Before we even walked out of the parking lot, she asked the manager for an application — filled it out right there, quick and neat — and handed it back to me to give to the manager.

My manager looked at me and asked, "Can you work third shift?"
I said yes.
Even though I wasn't sure I could.
Then she asked if she could call later that evening.
I said yes again — shocked she was even considering me.
As we walked back to the car, her belly pressed against the steering wheel.
She looked at me with that quiet confidence she always carried.

Everywhere we went, she pushed me forward.
She wanted me to succeed.
She wanted a better life for us.
She wanted me to be more than what the world expected from a kid like me.
We agreed I should work nights.
The hours were long, but it meant I could be with her during the day at her aunt's house.
A system.
A routine.
Something that looked like a family trying to build a life.
So after leaving the hospital, I went to work.
Ready to grind.
Ready to do whatever I had to do.
I wanted us to have a home — our first place — and I wanted to get it myself.
And eventually, I did.
But what I didn't know was this:
The past I thought I escaped…
Was still alive.
Still in the system.
Still attached to my name.
Still waiting.
And soon enough—
It caught up to me.
Harder than I could've imagined.

TRANSITIONING

The next morning, I got off work the same way I always did—
Eyes burning from a long night.
Clothes smelling like fryers and sweat.
Body heavy from standing twelve hours straight.
But this morning felt different.
I walked toward the bus stop slowly, half-dragging my feet, half-lost in my thoughts.
I stopped at the corner store like usual and grabbed a snack and a drink.
It felt good — good — to finally have a little money in my pocket.
I'd been at that job for a few months now.
I wasn't making much, but it was enough to feel something I had never felt before:
Not broke.
I didn't even know what being "a man" really meant.
But having money to buy things I wanted — and money to give to my son's mother so she could buy what she felt she needed for her and the baby —
That made me feel like I was stepping into something real.
And that day, I did something I had never done before.
I asked the clerk for a cigar.
I had turned eighteen without even realizing how fast time moved.
Life had hit fast-forward.
Everyone around me smoked, drank, or did something to take the edge off.
If I was twenty-one, honestly, I might've grabbed a beer too.
My mind was spinning.
I was a dad now.
Every emotion hit at once.
But the one I tried hardest to drown — the one I refused to let swallow me —
Was the fear that I wouldn't be a good father.
That I wouldn't be there.
That her family might take the baby and disappear.

That I'd end up like the men arguing on porches —
Complaining about child support.
Cussing out their baby mamas.
Saying they were blocked from seeing their kids.
Where I came from, that was normal.
Almost expected.
And I couldn't shake it.
No matter how much I knew she wasn't like that.
Everything she had done for me —
She wasn't that kind of girl.
Still… doubt creeps in even when you know better.
I stepped outside, unwrapped the cigar, lit it, and took the smallest pull.
My whole chest caught on fire.
I coughed so hard my eyes watered.
Either God was teaching me something quick,
Or that cigar was just trash.
Maybe both.
I dropped it to the ground and stepped on it.
First and last time.
I kept walking.
Wiping my eyes.
Heading to the bus stop.
Heading to the hospital.
Heading into whatever this new life was about to be.
A young father.
Still a kid inside.
Trying to grow up fast enough to keep up with a world that didn't slow down for anybody.
When I made it to the hospital, her aunt was already there.
The door was halfway open. I could hear bags zipping, plastic crinkling, soft voices trying not to wake the baby.
They were packing up.
Discharge day.
This was the moment of truth.
I stepped in and went straight into helping.

Her aunt gave me a tired smile.
"How was work?"
"Long," I said.
It was always long.
She knew that.
I knew that.
It was small talk — but I could feel her watching me.
Measuring me.
Trying to see if I was serious about this life.
Then she asked,
"You want to ride with us to the house?"
Before I could think, my son's mother looked at me.
Say yes.
So I did.
"Yeah. I'll ride with y'all."
I picked up my son — tiny, warm, wrapped tight —
And everything slowed down.
But before we stepped out, I looked back at the hospital bed.
The folded blanket.
The empty baby bin.
And the doubts crept back in.
Had I missed something the night before?
Should I have stayed?
Should I have said more?
Those thoughts followed me into the hallway.
And that's when I saw it.
The chair.
The one her father sat in the night my son was born.
Empty.
But heavy.
I could still see his face.
That look.
Judgment.
Disappointment.
Maybe fear of what kind of man I was.
Seeing that chair felt like reliving it all.

But I kept walking.
Outside, we walked toward her aunt's car.
Every step felt heavier.
Not because of my son.
Because I had to get this right.
I didn't have a father.
I didn't have a blueprint.
I only had responsibility.
We got in.
The ride was quiet at first.
Then her aunt said,
"You tired?"
"Yeah."
"You must rest when you can. It's different now. Everything different."
She was right.
I watched the hospital disappear behind us.
The city rolled by.
The bus stops.
The streets I used to survive on.
Now I wasn't surviving alone.
I was somebody's father.
Halfway there, she said softly,
"I'm proud of y'all."
Then corrected herself.
"I'm proud of you. Both of you."
Nobody had ever said that to me in a moment like that.
I didn't know how to respond.
So I didn't.
I just looked at my son and let it sit in my chest.
Hope.
Fear.
Responsibility.
Pride.
All at once.
Back Door

We pulled up to her aunt's house.
A steep incline leading to the backyard.
Grass overgrown.
Ground uneven.
Her aunt's husband never cut it.
We always went through the back door.
The small dog barked as soon as we stepped onto the porch.
It never went outside.
Just moved from room to room depending on who complained that day.
The yard looked like it was surviving the weather.
Just like us.
We went inside.
The Hallway That Held Everything
The layout was simple.
Everything connected through one narrow hallway:
• Her aunt's room
• A half-working bathroom
• The kitchen
• The living room
• The old dog room
• And finally, the room where she and our son stayed
Everyone walked that hallway.
Every sound traveled through it.
Every smell.
Every argument.
Every conversation.
It was the spine of the house.
I didn't live there.
I wasn't allowed to spend the night.
I came during the day.
Left when her aunt said it was time.
But even in daylight, I saw what we were up against.
Her Room — My Son's First Home
Small.
Bed against the wall.

Baby bags stacked in the corner.
Carpet still faintly smelling like the dog.
Dim light.
Door that barely closed.
This was where she would raise our son until we figured something out.
We didn't have much:

- Two boxes of diapers
- Some wipes
- A few baby clothes
- A hand-me-down blanket

But she didn't complain.
Not once.
She laid him down gently and dressed him in a little blue onesie that said, "Momma Boy."
Watching her do that made everything real.
This wasn't the life we imagined.
But it was the life we had.
Trying to Help
I couldn't give her a house.
Couldn't give her a car.
Couldn't give her stability yet.
But I gave what I could.
"You want me to cut the front yard?" I asked her aunt one day.
She looked surprised.
Like nobody had offered in years.
She said yes.
So I pushed that half-broken mower up and down that steep hill until the yard looked like it had a chance.
It wasn't much.
But sometimes something is enough.
Ant
Later, her aunt divorced and remarried a man named Ant.
Short.
Cool.
Positive.

The kind of man who tried to see good in people.
Her parents didn't like him.
Just like they didn't like me.
But her grandmother did.
And Ant talked to me about work.
About fatherhood.
About responsibility.
He saw potential in me when I barely saw any in myself.
That mattered.

Nights and Days

Working nights and showing up during the day became my routine.
Get off work.
Long bus ride.
Walk up that hill.
Back door.
Hold my son.
Even when my body wanted to collapse.
Sometimes I'd sit on the edge of the bed, and my head would drop without me knowing.
She'd whisper,
"You tired… you should sleep."
But where was I supposed to sleep?
So I stayed.
Until her aunt said it was time for me to go.
Then I'd walk back down that hill.
Back into the night.
Back into whatever few hours of rest I could find before my shift.
Some nights I felt like I wasn't living.
Just switching roles:

- Father in the day
- Worker at night
- Survivor in between

But every time I held my son —
Every blink.
Every yawn.

Every small smile in his sleep —
I knew I had something worth fighting for.
And that's what kept me going.

UNEXPECTED CHALLENGES

The approval call came while I was sitting at the transit station, staring down at my shoes, thinking about everything it took to get here.

The realtor's voice was calm, almost emotionless.

"You've been approved for the duplex."

Just like that.

A sentence that changed everything.

I called her immediately.

"We got approved," I said.

For a moment, she didn't respond.

No excitement.

No relief.

Just silence.

"You there?" I asked.

"Yes," she finally said — but not the way I imagined.

Her voice was soft.

Distant.

Like she was holding something in.

"What's wrong?" I asked.

She didn't answer that.

Instead, she said:

"When are you coming to get us?"

Those words hit harder than the approval.

I wasn't just getting a place.

I was getting a family.

"I'm on the way," I told her.

I rushed to the bus stop.

Mind racing.

Heart pounding.

The ride felt long, but the walk from the stop to her grandmother's house felt even longer.

The same church sat on the corner — the one I always passed but never entered.

This time, I stopped.

Looked up.
And whispered,
"Thank you."
No anger.
No questions.
Just gratitude.
For a moment I never thought I'd reach.
When I got to her grandmother's house, she was already stepping outside — purse on her shoulder, keys in her hand.
"Hey Idris," she said.
"They are inside. Your son and his momma. How are you doing?"
"I'm alright."
Then she asked if I knew anything about cars — her tire pressure light had come on.
"Maybe you got a nail," I said.
She jumped.
"A nail? In new tires?"
I didn't know what else to say.
Then the door opened.
She stepped out.
Holding our newborn son wrapped tight in a hospital blanket.
Both arms locked around him.
Protective.
Careful.
For a moment, we just stared at each other.
No words.
Just the understanding of two young parents stepping into a life neither of us was ready for.
Her grandmother asked if we needed anything.
Asked if we needed a ride.
Pride made me lie.
"No ma'am, we are good."
Even though we weren't.
We walked to the bus stop.
Her first time ever riding a bus.
My world.

Not hers.
When the bus pulled up, the driver waved us in fast.
"Y'all got that beautiful baby out here — hurry on now!"
Inside, she looked around like she had stepped into another universe.
She never had to ride buses.
Never had to count transfers.
Never had to memorize routes.
Our worlds were blending.
She held our son the entire ride.
Never loosened her grip.
Never asked for help.
Just steady.
Strong.
All I could think about was the route.
The transfer.
The stop.
But underneath that…
A whisper I didn't want to admit:
The lights.
The gas.
The bills.
I didn't have the money.
At the transit center, I froze.
The bus we needed arrived.
Left.
Arrived again.
Left again.
She didn't complain.
Didn't rush me.
Just sat on the blue bench, rocking our son gently.
Finally, she asked:
"Did you forget the bus number?"
Not annoyed.
Just calm.
I stood up like I was about to walk.

But my feet wouldn't move.

My chest tightened.

I looked at her.

Her tired but glowing face.

Our son sleeping.

And I said it.

"I'm out of money. I don't have enough for the lights or the gas."

She didn't panic.

Didn't blame me.

Didn't cry.

She just processed it.

Then reached into her purse.

Still holding our son with one arm.

She pulled out her phone.

Called her father.

I didn't hear everything.

But I heard enough in her tone…

To know he didn't like the call.

When she hung up, she sat quietly.

Then said,

"He wants to meet us at the place."

I nodded.

"Alright. Text him the address."

She typed:

We'll be there in about an hour.

Then held our son even closer.

While we waited, something strange happened.

A man walked into the transit station.

Didn't speak.

Didn't look around.

Didn't explain anything.

He just walked through handing envelopes to people sitting on benches.

I ignored him.

Until he tapped my shoulder.

He handed me one.

And walked away.
No words.
I opened it expecting a church flyer.
Instead—
Money.
Enough to turn on the lights.
Not the gas.
Not everything.
But the lights.
The one thing I was afraid to admit we didn't have.
By the time I looked up—
He was gone.
Vanished into the crowd.
She looks at me with a face of faith like she knew something good would happen.
Eventually our bus pulled up.
We got on.
She held our son steady.
Strong.
Unshaken.
I held the envelope like something sacred.
And for the first time that day—
I knew we were going home.

UNEXPECTED HELP

The walk from the bus stop to the duplex was only three minutes.
But it felt longer with everything sitting on my chest.
When we turned the corner, I saw him immediately.
Her father.
Standing outside his car.
Not leaning.
Not distracted.
Just facing the road.
Watching the direction we walked from.
Like he already knew we came on the bus.
She stepped toward him first, our son held tight in her arms. When she got close enough, he hugged them both.
That surprised me.
Then his eyes shifted to me.
No words.
No greeting.
Just a look.
I walked toward the duplex door, him following behind me. His footsteps were slow. Heavy.
My stomach tightened.
She knew about the lights.
She knew I hadn't paid the deposit.
She knew I didn't have the money.
She knew we were stepping into uncertainty.
But her father didn't know any of that.
All he knew was she had called him and said,
"We got a place."
I put the key in the lock.
I expected darkness.
Expected the switch not to work.
Expected humiliation.
I turned the knob.
Stepped inside.

Flipped the switch.
The light came on.
Bright.
Steady.
I froze.
Her father stepped in behind me, walking slowly through the empty living room.
No couch.
No mattress.
No blanket.
No pillow.
Just bare floors and cold air.
She walked in holding our son close.
She didn't complain.
Didn't question it.
She accepted the house for what it was:
Ours.
Her father stopped in the middle of the room.
"This where you are going' to stay?"
His voice wasn't loud.
But it carried weight.
She answered softly.
"Yes."
He looked around again.
Then at me.
Then at her.
"Alright," he said.
"It's your life."
He walked toward the door and opened it halfway.
"Let me talk to you."
She handed me our son — the first time I held him that day — and followed her father outside.
The door closed.
Silence filled the house.
I leaned against the wall and slowly slid down to the floor, holding my son tight.

His little face looked up at me.
Peaceful.
Unaware.
My breath shook.
Tears came without warning.
Not because she didn't believe in me.
She did.
Not because we had nothing.
I was used to that.
But because this was real.
I was a father.
I had a home.
I had a family.
And all I had to offer was effort.
I heard a car engine start.
For a second, I thought they were leaving.
Forty minutes later, headlights flashed through the window.
They were back.
She stepped out carrying two bags — clothes, a sheet, a blanket, personal things.
Her father walked around to the back of the car holding a queen-size air mattress still in the box.
He didn't say anything.
Didn't lecture.
Didn't ask questions.
Didn't mention heat.
He just carried the mattress inside and set it on the floor.
Then he kissed her forehead.
Walked out.
Drove away.
No speech.
Just provision.
We carried the box into the bedroom.
Opened it.
Pulled the folded mattress onto the floor.

The small pump hummed loudly, filling the empty house with sound — making it feel less lonely.
Slowly, the mattress rose.
Our first piece of furniture.
We stretched the sheet over it.
Pulled the blanket across.
She unwrapped our son and laid him gently in the center.
Not in a hospital blanket.
But in one she brought from home.
Soft.
Light.
Ours.
She sat on one side.
I sat on the other.
No heat.
No furniture.
No comfort except each other.
The air was cool but not freezing.
Just enough to pull the blanket higher.
I lay back and stared at the ceiling.
Listening.
Her breathing.
His tiny breaths.
The house settling around us.
And for the first time in my life…
I felt like I had a family.
A real one.
Nothing else mattered that night.
Not the empty rooms.
Not the fear.
Not the struggle waiting outside those walls.
Just us.
On an air mattress.
In a cold house.
That we could finally call home.

A HOUSE WITHOUT HEAT

For the first week in our new home, we lived without gas.
No heat.
No hot water.
But home
And it wasn't winter yet — just cool at night. Not harsh. Not painful. Just enough to remind us we started with nothing.
Every evening, when the sky turned orange and blue, I got dressed for work. She sat on the air mattress with our son resting against her chest, both was wrapped in the blanket her father brought.
The house wasn't warm — but it was ours.
Leaving every night hit me in a strange way.
Half of me felt proud —
like I was doing something right,
like I was stepping into fatherhood,
like I was providing, even if it wasn't much.
The other half was doubt.
What if she leaves?
What if I can't do this?
What if I fail like the men before me?
Those thoughts followed me from the front door to the bus stop.
The nights weren't cold — just breezy.
But the pressure inside me was heavier than the air.
At work, the smell of taco meat and fryer oil hit me in the face.
Third shift was always the same — loud headsets, sizzling pans, orders stacking up.
No burgers.
No grills.
Just tacos, chalupas, quesadillas, nachos.
Sometimes, assembling tacos back-to-back, my mind drifted home.
Were they okay?
Was she lonely?
Was the baby warm enough?
Was she second-guessing me?

On break, I'd sit behind the building near the dumpsters — the only quiet spot.
One more week, I told myself.
One more week until payday.
One more week until I could pay the gas deposit.
One more week until it felt stable.
The lights were already on — thanks to that stranger at the transit station.
But without gas, the house felt unfinished.
When my shift ended, the sky would be turning gray. The walk back to the duplex always felt calm.
And when I opened the door —
There they were.
She asleep on her side.
Our son wrapped tight beside her.
The room cool but not uncomfortable.
Seeing them like that every morning settled something in me.
For the first time in my life, standing in a quiet room at sunrise, I felt this:
I can build this.
I can grow into this.
I can be better than what I came from.
We didn't have heat.
We didn't have furniture.
But we had peace.
And peace was something I had never owned before.
Every night I left, I felt two things at once:
Relief that they were inside a home.
Fear that I wouldn't hold it together.
That fear came from my past — all the instability, all the disappearing.
Now I had something I never had before.
A family.
And the fear of losing it beat in my chest like a second heartbeat.
Still, I kept walking to that bus stop.
Kept coming home exhausted.

We were building something from nothing.

And even though the house was empty, it was ours.

The Bottle Warmer

One morning, after only an hour of sleep, she woke me gently.

"The bottle warmer isn't working."

No microwave. No gas.

"He's going to have to drink cold milk."

I sat up immediately.

We didn't have much. That warmer was one of the few things we depended on.

"Give me the bottle," I said.

I stepped outside into the cool morning air and looked around.

A car pulled into the driveway next door. A woman in her forties stepped out carrying groceries.

I walked over and knocked.

When she opened the door, her face reminded me of my mother on her good days — soft, patient.

I told her everything that mattered at the moment.

Broken warmer. No gas. Need warm milk.

She didn't question me.

"Come in."

Her house felt lived in — pictures, warm colors, kids' voices somewhere in the back.

She warmed the bottle in her microwave.

"You the new neighbor?"

"Yes ma'am."

"I didn't see a moving truck."

"We're just waiting on furniture."

She handed me the bottle.

"If you ever need help, just knock."

I thanked her and walked back.

She watched me for a second longer than necessary.

Like she understood.

Inside, I handed the bottle over. She smiled with relief and fed our son.

That was fatherhood for me then —

Work.
Survive.
Repeat.
No applause.
Just responsibility.
The Manager Who Saw Through Me
That night, my manager was there.
"There he goes — my strong one."
I never felt strong.
In jail, I cried.
Without my mother, I felt empty.
Growing up, I felt unseen.
But she spoke to me like she saw something.
She asked about the house.
"Your family bring housewarming gifts?"
"It's coming together," I said.
She asked about the baby.
I told her the truth — we were waiting to turn the gas on when I got paid.
She shook her head gently.
"You a kid doing grown-man work. But you are doing it."
We worked through the night.
When morning came, she called me over.
I thought I messed up the register.
Instead, she opened it and pulled out a $100 bill.
Folded it once.
Placed it in my hand.
"You know what you need it for."
No pity.
No lecture.
Just help.
She didn't see a failure.
She saw a man trying.
I whispered, "Thank you."
Walked to the bus stop with that $100 in my pocket and my chest tight.

Now I had enough to turn the gas on.
Enough to give my son warm bottles in our own house.
Enough to make our start feel real.
Enough for hope.

QUALITIES I NEEDED

A whole year passed inside that little duplex before I even realized it.

No eviction notices.

No social workers knocking.

No sudden disaster waiting outside the window.

Just… life settling in.

Simple life.

My son was one now — wobbling into corners, laughing when he fell like the floor was part of the game.

His mother adjusted to motherhood with a calmness I always admired. She made a home out of almost nothing.

Me?

Still working nights.

Still catching the bus home at sunrise.

Still trying to build something steady out of a life that had never been steady.

Slowly, piece by piece, our place started looking real:

- A real bed — not air.
- A cheap TV.
- A microwave that worked just enough.

Those small things felt big.

They made the house feel lived in.

They made me feel like I was providing.

We didn't have much.

A few bags of clothes.

A donated crib.

A couch from the curb.

Just enough food to get through the week.

But for a while, it was okay.

She lived what she saw growing up — routine, structure, early mornings, cleaning, cooking, caring. Stability was normal to her.

I lived what I thought a man was supposed to be.

Pieces from everywhere:

Uncles talking tough.
Neighborhood hustlers.
Gang dudes bragging.
My grandfather barking orders.
My mother's husband drifting in and out.
And then there was her father.
The man who didn't like me.
The man I didn't like much either.
But he had something none of the men around me ever had:
Consistency.
Discipline.
Responsibility.
Pride in protecting his household.
Structure that didn't bend.
He wasn't perfect.
But he was present.
He stood firm.
He led without chaos.
And that bothered me at first — because I couldn't ignore it.
I didn't want to be him.
But I wanted what he represented.
The disciplined version of manhood.
Watching him from a distance — stubborn, quiet, pretending I didn't care — shaped something in me.
It taught me something I never heard growing up:
Providing isn't loud.
It's not tough talk.
It's not fear.
It's not street survival.
It's showing up.
Every day.
When you're tired.
When you're scared.
When you don't know if you're doing it right.
That year inside that duplex wasn't dramatic.
It wasn't flashy.

But it was the beginning of something new.
The beginning of me choosing discipline over survival.
Structure over chaos.
Presence over pride.
The beginning of becoming someone my son's mother could trust.
Someone my son could one day look at and say:
That's what a man is.

I STAND, I FALL

There comes a point in a man's life where the mirror stops showing a face
and starts showing a question.
For me, that question started the day I realized I wasn't "Idress" anymore.
Not to the world.
Not on paper.
Not to landlords.
Not to managers.
Not to anyone holding a form in their hands.
On paper, I was a felon.
A conspiracy charge that never told the full story
but followed me louder than my name ever did.
Every application.
Every interview.
Every lease.
Have you ever been convicted of a felony?
That question carried more weight than my entire life.
And no matter how hard I worked,
that word — felony — entered the room before I did.
At home, I had a family.
A woman who chose me.
A son who smiled at me like I was already enough.
But inside?
I was cracking.
Eight dollars an hour.
Night shift.
Little sleep.
Bills stacking faster than paychecks.
Food stamps stretching thin.
Bus rides stealing hours from my body.
Some days I felt like I was holding everything together with my fingertips.

One night, when the pressure got too loud,
I sat her down.
"I got to tell you something."
She looked at me like she already felt it coming.
"I got a record," I said.
"A felony. That's why it's hard. Jobs. Apartments. Everything."
I swallowed.
"People don't see me. They see what the paper says."
She didn't move away.
She moved closer.
"I don't see you that way," she said softly.
"I know who you are."
That should've brought peace.
But it scared me.
Because I didn't know who I was becoming.
I was stuck between two versions of myself:
The boy who survived chaos.
And the man trying to build stability out of nothing.
After long shifts, I'd sit on the edge of the bed in the dark
listening to my son as he breathes.
Silence makes fear louder.
Bills.
Pressure.
Expectations.
My past knocking.
My future depending on me.
Some nights I felt strong.
Some nights I felt like I was one bad moment away from breaking.
Most nights I felt both.
Standing for my family.
Falling under the weight of becoming the man I needed to be.
I didn't want my son to grow up wondering who his father was.
I wanted him to know I fought.
Even when I was unsure.
Even when I was tired.
Even when I was afraid.

In the quiet darkness, I'd whisper to myself:
"You can't fall now."
And slowly I started understanding something I never understood before:
Falling isn't failure.
Staying down is.
This was the chapter where I learned the truth:
A man becomes a man
in the moments he feels most unsure of himself.
And every night…
I was learning who that man was supposed to be.

A WOMAN WORTH

There are women who walk into your life,
and there are women who hold it together.
She was the second kind.
Not loud.
Not dramatic.
Not demanding.
Just steady.
Present.
Solid in a way I didn't fully understand back then,
because I was too busy trying to keep myself upright.
She saw the cracks in me before I admitted they existed.
Saw the weight on my shoulders when I tried to hide it.
Saw the fear in my eyes when I thought about rent,
about bills,
about being the father I never had.
And she didn't run.
She leaned in.
There were days the world made me feel like less of a man—
Job applications rejected.
Apartments denying us.
"Felony" thrown at me like a label instead of a lesson.
But she never used it against me.
Not once.
Instead, she looked at me like she saw a man
I hadn't grown into yet
but believed I would.
She was patient in ways I didn't always deserve.
Quiet when I needed quiet.
Firm when I started slipping.
Gentle when shame made me pull away.
Some mornings after long night shifts,
I'd walk in exhausted,
eyes heavy, mind spinning.
I'd fall onto the bed barely able to think.
She'd tuck the blanket around me and whisper,

"Go to sleep. I got him."

She didn't compete with my struggle.

She didn't pressure me to move faster than I could.

She didn't question whether I could be a father.

She just showed up.

Every day.

Even when she was tired too.

One afternoon, after I got home from work, she waited until I sat down.

"My aunt said she'll watch our son… if I get a job," she said.

For a second, I froze.

A job?

Her working?

I didn't know what I felt—

pride, fear, relief, insecurity.

Maybe all of it.

"You… get a job?" I asked.

She smiled — that quiet, shy smile she made when she was serious but didn't want to sound bold.

"Yes," she said. "I can work."

"Where?"

"I want to be a CNA," she said. "The classes are free for women with kids."

I didn't even know what that meant at the time.

"A what?"

"A nurse," she laughed.

We didn't even have a computer.

She found out through her aunt.

And in that moment, I realized something:

While I was fighting to survive,

she was thinking about building.

A different level of strength.

A different level of vision.

Part of me was scared.

They were my peace.

Seeing them when I got off work kept me grounded.

But she looked ready.
Confident.
Certain in a way I hadn't seen before.
So I said,
"Okay. If you want to do it, do it. I got you."
And she smiled — not small this time, but full.
That smile said more than words.
A woman worth something doesn't just love you.
She builds with you.
She steadies you.
She sees who you can become
without trying to control who you are.
She didn't save me.
She reminded me I wasn't broken beyond repair.
Looking back now, I understand something I couldn't see then:
A woman worth having
is the one who stands steady
while you're still becoming.
And she did.
Long before I learned how to do the same.

CROSSING PATHS

The first week of her classes changed everything.

Not in a dramatic way.

Not in a fight.

Not in an explosion.

Just in silence.

I didn't expect how different the house would feel when I woke up and she wasn't there.

Most mornings, sunlight would hit the wall, and I'd realize I had missed them by hours. She was already dressed, already gone, already stepping into something new. The quiet didn't feel sad — it felt unfamiliar. The house wasn't empty.

It was adjusting.

Her aunt came every morning to pick her up. Dropped her off every afternoon too. No bus stops. No transfers. No long waits in the cold. No standing under flickering streetlights wondering if the next ride would come.

She had support.

Real support.

And I was glad for that. I didn't want her struggling the way I had. But still…

Something twisted inside me every time I saw her aunt's car pull into the driveway. Every time I watched them talk before she got in. Every time she walked out wearing her bookbag, confident, moving toward a future that had structure.

It wasn't jealousy.

It was fear.

Fear that she had something solid behind her.

Fear that if she ever stepped back and compared her world to mine, the difference would be obvious.

Fear that in those car rides they were talking about me.

Quietly.

Honestly.

Truthfully.

Some mornings I stood behind the curtain, watching the car disappear down the street, asking myself questions I never said out loud:
What if they don't think I'm good enough?
What if she starts believing them?
What if she outgrows me while I'm still fighting my past?
I worked seven nights a week.
She trained five days a week.
My world ran under streetlights.
Hers ran under daylight.
We barely crossed paths anymore.
Some days it was just a quick kiss in the doorway. A tired smile. A handoff of our son. Then one of us leaving while the other stayed.
No arguments.
No accusations.
Just distance.
She was growing.
And I felt like I was holding my ground, trying not to slide backward.
When she came home from class, exhausted but proud, talking about what she learned — medical terms I didn't understand, patient stories, instructors correcting her posture — I listened.
I nodded.
I smiled.
But inside, something shifted.
She had people guiding her forward.
I had only myself.
Late at night, on the bus ride home, I would stare out the window and let the thoughts run:
What if one day she realizes I'm still carrying everything from before?
What if I lose her not because I failed… but because she evolved?
What if I become the chapter she outgrows?
I didn't know how to say any of that without sounding insecure.
So I didn't say it at all.
I stayed quiet.

Worked harder.
Slept less.
Held my son tighter.
Hoped more.
This wasn't a breakup.
It wasn't anger.
It wasn't betrayal.
It was something quieter.
Something slower.
The kind of distance that forms when two people love each other but live on different clocks.
And deep down, I felt it.
A storm was forming.
Not outside the house.
Not in the streets.
Not in the bills.
Inside us.
Inside me.
I was no longer the boy trying to survive.
I was a man trying to build.
But building something stable requires more than effort.
It requires identity.
And I was still figuring out who I was becoming.
The woman beside me was stepping into her purpose.
The child between us was growing fast.
And me?
I was standing at the edge of something I didn't fully understand yet.
The past hadn't finished with me.
The future was arriving faster than I could prepare for it.
And somewhere in the space between who I had been and who I needed to become…
I realized something:
Love isn't what tests a man.
Growth does.

And I was about to find out
whether I could grow
without losing everything I built.
That's where the next chapter truly begins.

For My Mother

Some people only see the mistakes.
But I saw everything the world never paused long enough to notice.

I saw the woman who kept trying even when life hit her harder than any one person should ever be hit.
I saw the mother who screamed my name that morning — not out of anger, but out of fear, out of love, out of something deeper than breath.
A scream pulled from her soul, a sound only a mother can make when she's losing the one thing she's been trying to hold together.

I saw the battles you fought in silence —
the ones that swallowed you whole,
the ones you carried alone while the world judged you from a distance,
the ones that crushed you long before anyone understood the weight you were lifting.

And I saw more than just you.

I saw every mother like you —
the mothers who break quietly behind closed doors,
the mothers who raise children while healing wounds no one knows about,
the mothers who give what they can while carrying pain they never asked for,
the mothers who love imperfectly but fiercely,
the mothers who show up even when they have nothing left to give.

This page is not here to blame you.
It's here to honor you —
and honor them.
All the women who loved through storms nobody else survived.

Because even in your brokenness, you were still my mother.
Even when life dimmed your light, you were still trying to give me

whatever pieces of warmth you had left.
Even in the moments you fell short, I could still feel the parts of you that loved me in the only ways you knew how.

And when the world judged you, I remembered the moments that made me feel seen.
The moments that told me I mattered.
The moments where you tried — even if it was small, even if it was brief, even if it got lost inside everything else.

This book carries parts of your story too.
Your wounds shaped the man I became.
Your absence sharpened my vision.
Your struggles taught me empathy I didn't have words for as a child.
Your survival — even when it was messy — built the foundation I had to climb out of.

And if you ever read these pages…
if your eyes ever fall on these words…
I want you to hear this truth without hesitation, without fear, without doubt:

I never stopped being your son.

ILOVE YOU

For My Children

To my children —
You will never have to grow up in the world I came from.
Your father walked through fire so you could walk on steady ground.
Every page of this book is a piece of the road I had to survive so you could have a road worth walking.

I want you to know this:
Your father didn't break.
Your father didn't fold.
Your father climbed out of a life that tried to bury him so you would never have to feel the things I felt.

You are my peace.
You are my new beginning.
You are the reason I built a life with structure, order, and meaning.

For My Family and Friends

To the ones who stayed,
To the ones who tried,
To the ones who saw pieces of me even when my world was falling apart…

Thank you.

Some of you helped me directly.
Some of you helped me without knowing it.
Some of you walked with me through seasons I didn't have the language to explain yet.

This book isn't written from blame — it's written from understanding.
Every person in my life became part of the map that brought me here.

If you were part of my childhood, my teenage years, or the early pieces of my adulthood…
you helped build the man who stands here today.

And for that, I honor you.

Why I Wrote This Book

I wrote this book because silence never saved me.
Silence kept me trapped in my own head, replaying memories that had nowhere to go.
Survival kept me alive — but survival without reflection becomes its own kind of prison.
I needed to take my story out of my chest and put it into words so nobody else would drown in the same kind of darkness I had to climb out of.

I wrote this book because too many boys grow up like I did and never get a chance to say what they lived through.
They walk through chaos without guidance.
They face systems without explanation.
They search for love in places that only teach them pain.
Nobody gives them a language for what they're feeling.
Nobody gives them a blueprint.

This book is my story the beginning.

I wrote this book because my struggle didn't end when my childhood ended — it followed me into adulthood.
It shaped the father I eventually became.
It shaped the man I chose to become.
It shaped the principles, discipline, and structure that built my entire foundation.
Every step I take today is connected to the boy who survived yesterday.

I wrote this book because I owed my younger self a voice.
He went through things no kid should ever have to see, feel, or carry.
I owed him a chance to be understood.
To be heard.
To be remembered with dignity instead of shame.

I wrote this book because I owed the world honesty.
Not a polished story.
Not a perfect sequence of events.

Not a movie script designed to entertain.
This book isn't meant to be flawless — it's meant to be true.

Not every character name is 100% real.
Not every scene is recreated with 100% accuracy.
Some details were changed to protect people, families, and situations.
But the heart of this story, the experiences, the emotions, the trauma, and the truth —
those are all mine.
Those are real.

And let me say this clearly:

This is not the end of my story.
This is only Book One.

There is more I need to tell —
more lessons,
more chapters,
more truth,
more growth,
more scars,
more healing.

The next book will continue what this one started.
Because my life didn't end when the pages stop —
and neither does the story.

I wrote this book for the kid I was…
and the man I became…
and for anyone out there who needs proof that broken beginnings don't mean broken endings.

ABOUT THE AUTHOR

Jocquill Bethea was born and raised in North Carolina and came of age in an environment shaped by instability, generational trauma, and systems that often failed young men before they ever had a chance.

From foster care to juvenile detention, from homelessness to early fatherhood, his life reflects the realities many experience but few speak about openly.

Labeled early.

Misunderstood often.

Defined by paperwork more than potential.

But labels did not finish his story.

Through resilience, reflection, and a deliberate commitment to becoming the father and man he never had, Jocquill rebuilt his life piece by piece.

He writes not as a motivational voice, but as a witness — to survival, to accountability, to growth.

This book is the first installment in a multi-part memoir series exploring identity, manhood, responsibility, loss, and transformation.

He writes for young men raised without guidance.

For those who survived on instinct.

For anyone who has ever felt invisible, misjudged, or written off too soon.

Jocquill Bethea's story is not about perfection.

It is about endurance.

And what happens when a man chooses to stand — even after he has fallen.

TailorMind Publishers

Founded by Jocquill Bethea

*"I wrote my book alone. I built my system alone.
I can help you do the same."*

TailorMind Publishers was built the same way this book was built — from nothing but discipline, clarity, and a refusal to quit.
Born out of struggle and rebuilt through purpose, TailorMind exists for writers who come from broken places, loud worlds, quiet hurts, and unfinished stories.

We publish with intention.
We protect the author's voice.
We honor the journey that shaped the story.

Every book that carries the TailorMind name is created with structure, honesty, and human care — not shortcuts, not noise, not trends.
Just truth, written cleanly and presented with excellence.

If this book reached you, then TailorMind did what it was created to do.

submissions@TailorMindPublishers.com

www.ingramcontent.com/pod-product-compliance
Lightning Source LLC
LaVergne TN
LVHW090514110826
845146LV00003B/850

* 9 7 9 8 9 9 4 9 9 4 5 0 4 *